ADA MINIMANUAL

to Accompany Appleby: Programming Languages: Paradigm and Practice

Also available from McGraw-Hill

SCHAUM'S OUTLINE SERIES IN COMPUTERS

Most outlines include basic theory, definitions, and hundreds of solved problems and supplementary problems with answers. Titles on the current list include:

Advanced Structured Cobol

Boolean Algebra

Computer Graphics

Computer Science

Computers and Business

Computers and Programming

Data Processing

Data Structures

Digital Principles, 2d edition

Discrete Mathematics

Essential Computer Mathematics

Linear Algebra, 2d edition

Mathematical Handbook of
    Formulas & Tables

Matrix Operations

Microprocessor Fundamentals,
    2d edition

Programming with Advanced
    Structured Cobol

Programming with Assembly
    Language

Programming with Basic,
    2d edition

Programming with C

Programming with Fortran

Programming with Pascal

Programming with Structured
    Cobol

SCHAUM'S SOLVED PROBLEMS BOOKS

Each title in this series is a complete and expert source of solved problems containing thousands of problems with worked out solutions. Related titles on the current list include:

3000 Solved Problems in Calculus

2500 Solved Problems in Differential Equations

2000 Solved Problems in Discrete Mathematics

3000 Solved Problems in Linear Algebra

2000 Solved Problems in Numerical Analysis

Available at your College Bookstore. A complete listing of Schaum titles may be obtained by writing to: Schaum Division
                     McGraw-Hill, Inc.
                     Princeton Road, S-1
                     Hightstown, NJ 08520

ADA MINIMANUAL

to Accompany Appleby: Programming Languages: Paradigm and Practice

George A. Benjamin
Muhlenberg College

McGraw-Hill, Inc.
New York St. Louis San Francisco Auckland Bogotá Caracas
Lisbon London Madrid Mexico Milan Montreal New Delhi Paris
San Juan Singapore Sydney Tokyo Toronto

ADA MiniManual to Accompany Appleby: Programming Languages:
Paradigm and Practice

1 2 3 4 5 6 7 8 9 0 DOC DOC 9 0 9 8 7 6 5 4 3 2 1

ISBN 0-07-002578-9

This book was designed and electronically typeset in Palatino
and Univers by Professional Book Center
The editor was Eric M. Munson;
the production supervisor was Annette Mayeski.
Cover design was done by Terry Earlywine;
copyediting was done by P. J. Schemenauer;
text programming was done by Thomas M. Woolf,
The index was prepared by Mark Savage Indexing Services.
Project supervision was done by Business Media Resources.
R. R. Donnelley & Sons Company was printer and binder.

Trademarked products cited:
AT&T 3B2 and AT&T 3B15 are registered trademarks of AT&T
Meridian Ada is a trademark of Meridian Software Systems, Inc.
MS-DOS is a trademark of Microsoft Corporation
UNIX is a registered trademark of AT&T Bell Laboratories
Verdix is a registered trademark of Verdix Corporation
Ada is a registered trademark of the U.S. Government, Ada Joint Program Office

CONTENTS

PREFACE

The purpose of this Ada mini-manual is to provide experienced programmers with a tool for learning the Ada programming language. Such an audience needs a description of the language at a level that falls between a textbook for beginners and the offical U.S. government document which defines Ada in detail — *ANSI/MIL-STD-1815A, Reference Manual for the Ada Programming Language* (known as the *Language Reference Manual – LRM.*)

This manual does not replace the LRM but rather supplements it by describing the major features of Ada in a less formal, yet still accurate manner, with numerous examples of code. A complete index and full set of appendixes (from the LRM) make this a good reference for the working programmer.

The first chapter is intended to help the reader begin immediately writing Ada programs. The structure of a main procedure is described, along with the basic IO routines for reading input from a keyboard and writing output to a monitor.

The second chapter covers the formalisms used to describe the syntax of Ada and also the rules for forming language components such as integers, real numbers, and identifiers.

The remaining chapters cover the features of the language: data types, variables, expressions, operator precedence, procedures, functions, packages, generics, tasks, exceptions, etc.

The code appearing in the manual was tested on two different compilers: the Meridian Ada Compiler V4.1 for PC DOS Systems and the Verdix Ada Development System Version 5.5 for the AT&T 3B Family of Computers. Details on these compilers are available at the following addresses.

Meridian Software Systems, Inc.
10 Pasteur Street
Irvine, CA 92718
Ph: (714) 727-0700

Verdix Corporation
Sullyfield Business Park
14130-A Sullyfield Circle
Chantilly, VA 22021
Ph: (703) 378-7600

ACKNOWLEDGMENTS

I owe a debt of thanks to Doris Appleby of Marymount College for offering me the opportunity to work on this project and for her encouragement, advice, and helpful comments.

I am grateful to Muhlenberg College and in particular John Meyer and Donald Shive for providing me with the resources I needed to complete this work.

Final thanks are reserved for Rachel and Samantha who make it all worthwhile.

George A. Benjamin

1

GETTING STARTED WITH ADA

1.1 INTRODUCTION

Ada can be characterized as a general-purpose, strongly typed, block-struc-
tured, procedural programming language. These terms serve to emphasize its
similarity with languages such as Pascal, PL/1, and FORTRAN. However, Ada
also has distinguishing features marking it as an evolutionary advancement
over its predecessors. The designers of Ada provided support for many of the
goals of current software design methodology. These include information hiding, program modularity, and reusablity of code. Ada also supports concurrency, exception handling, and low-level, implementation-dependent features,
making it suitable for systems programming applications such as device drivers
and operating systems. In this chapter, Ada's similarities with other languages
are exploited in order to enable you to begin writing your own programs
quickly. Advanced features are discussed in later chapters.

The next section contains a short program illustrating the basic structure
of an Ada main program. This provides a foundation on which to build as you
learn additional features of the language. The chapter concludes with a description of the standard input and output library procedures and functions.

1.2 A SAMPLE PROGRAM

An Ada program typically consists of a *main procedure* in which execution
begins, along with a collection of program libraries, called *compilation units*,
which the main procedure uses. Here is a simple Ada program:

```
1      with Text_IO;   use Text_IO;
2
3      --
4      --   An Ada program that prints a greeting
5      --
6
7      procedure First is
8
9          Name  : String(1..40);      -- A string of 40 characters
10         Ch    : Character;          -- Used to read from input.
11         Index : Integer := 0;       -- An index into a string
12
13     begin
14         Put("What is your name? ");      -- Prompt for a name
15         while (not End_Of_Line) loop
16             Get(Ch);                     -- Read the name one
17             Index := Index + 1;          -- character at a time
18             Name(Index) := Ch;           -- up to a maximum of
19             exit when (Index = 40);  -- 40 characters.
20         end loop;
21         Skip_Line;
22         New_Line;
23         Put("Hello ");
24         Put_Line(Name(1..Index));
25     end First;
```

This is an interactive program that prompts the user for a name, reads the name from a line, and prints a personalized "Hello" greeting. The line numbers are not part of the program; they are included only so that the source text can be referenced.

A sample execution of the program is shown below. Input typed by the user is shown in boldface.

```
What is your name?  Ada Lovelace
Hello Ada Lovelace
```

The program exhibits some common conventions used in Ada program listings. Reserved words are printed in lowercase boldface, statements are listed one per line (although this is not required), and indentation is used to exhibit the structure of the program. There is one convention started in the *LRM* that is not followed in the example program (nor in the rest of this manual outside of the appendixes): printing identifiers which are not reserved words in uppercase (INTEGER, CHARACTER, PUT, etc.) For ease of reading, user identifiers are in lowercase, using capital letters for emphasis. In Ada, identifiers are not case sensitive.

Let's examine the program in detail.

Line 1

The program starts with a with clause.

```
with  Text_IO;
```

This tells the compiler that the program is going to use a program library, in this case `Text_IO`. `Text_IO` contains a collection of packages of code providing procedures that permit the input and output of data from a standard input device (usually a keyboard) and to a standard output device (usually a monitor). It is the most common library used. In our example, `Text_IO` provides the routines `Put`, `Put_Line`, `Get`, `Skip_Line`, `New_Line`, and `End_Of_Line`.

Normally the procedures provided by packages in a program library must have the name of the package as a prefix. Thus the `Put` procedure is more properly referred to as `Text_IO.Put`. The **use** clause:

```
use Text_IO;
```

makes the routines in `Text_IO` directly visible to the program without the need for the `Text_IO` prefix.

Lines 3–5

A comment begins with a double dash "--" and extends to the end of the line.

Line 7

The main procedure heading

```
procedure First is
```

declares the name of the program, `First`.

Lines 9–11

Declarations for the variables used by the program appear after the procedure heading. Ada is a strongly typed language and the type of data stored by each variable must be explicitly specified. The variable `Name` has type `String` and is essentially an array of 40 characters; `Ch` has type `Character` and can store a single character; `Index` has type `Integer` and can store a single whole number. The declaration of `Index` shows how Ada permits a variable to be initialized when it is declared.

The type names `String`, `Character`, and `Integer` are not reserved words. These types are defined in an Ada package called `Standard`. The `Standard` package must be available to all programs and the use of a **with** clause is not needed to access its provisions. Other types provided in `Standard` are `Boolean` and `Float`.

Line 13 and line 25

The reserved words **begin** in line 13 and **end** in line 25 bracket the statement section of the program.

Lines 14–24

This is such a simple program that it can be understood without additional comment, but a few observations are in order.

A semicolon, ";" , is used to terminate each statement; this is required. The while loop in lines 15 through 20 is provided with two conditions of termination — if the end of the input line is encountered or if the string variable Name is filled to capacity. New_Line is a procedure which terminates the current output line so that subsequent output appears on a new line. The procedure Put outputs data to the current line. Put_Line is similar to Put, but in addition terminates the line. Thus,

```
Put_Line("Hello");
```

is equivalent to

```
Put("Hello");
New_Line;
```

Get and Skip_Line are input procedures. Get reads data from input and Skip_Line causes any additional data on the current line to be ignored and skipped over.

The sample program First illustrates the general form of an Ada main procedure. There are three parts:

with clauses With clauses specify the program libraries that the procedure is going to use. Text_IO, for example, is used to provide IO services.

Declarations The declarations appear immediately after the procedure heading. This is where new data types (arrays, records, etc.), variables, and local procedures and functions are declared.

Statements The statement section comes after the declarations and is bracketed between the reserved words **begin** and **end**.

The formal structure for an Ada main procedure is:

```
with units;
use packages;
procedure program_name  is
     declarations -       including data types, variables,
                          procedures, and functions
begin
     statements
end   program_name;
```

1.3 STANDARD INPUT AND OUTPUT WITH `Text_IO`

`Text_IO` is a package of routines providing input and output on text files. It enables the use of text file variables and furnishes procedures and functions for reading and writing both character and numeric data. The package also supplies standard input and output files that are used by default when an IO routine does not specify a file parameter. These standard files are commonly associated with a keyboard (for input) and monitor (for output), but an execution environment may permit them to be disk files. An example of this is the use of IO redirection in the MS-DOS and UNIX operating systems.

This section shows how to use the procedures `Get` and `Put` to read and write `Character`, `String`, `Integer`, and `Float` (real number) data on Ada's standard text files. We also look at the procedures and functions which exploit the fact that these files can be organized into lines and pages. A further treatment of files is found in Chapter 10.

Accessing Text_IO

As the sample program of section 1.2 illustrated, a **with** clause is required to access `Text_IO` and a **use** clause allows the routines to be referenced without the `Text_IO` prefix. This is all that is needed for IO with the character-based types `Character` and `String`.

Numeric IO (reading and writing integers and real numbers) is implemented by generic packages within `Text_IO`. A generic package provides routines suitable for a general class of data. However, each specific data type in the class requires a different "instance" of the package. This is accomplished in Ada by a process called *instantiation*.

As an example, `Text_IO` contains a generic package called `Integer_IO` that has `Get` and `Put` procedures for reading and writing the general class of data we would call "whole numbers." However, a program may have variables of different "whole number" data types, such as `Byte`, for quantities restricted to the range 0 to 255, or `Integer` if there are no restrictions. Because Ada is strongly typed, `Get` and `Put` procedures that could accept parameters of type `Byte` could not accept parameters of type `Integer`. Even though variables of type `Byte` and `Integer` represent "whole numbers," they are different data types. What is needed are two "instances" of the `Get` and `Put` procedures for whole numbers: one for `Byte` and one for `Integer` data. Statements to instantiate the packages are:

```
package Int_IO is new Integer_IO(Integer);   use Int_IO;
package Byt_IO is new Integer_IO(Byte);      use Byt_IO;
```

These statements cause two packages (Int_IO and Byt_IO) to be generated from the generic Integer_IO package. The **use** clauses are not required but allow the Int_IO and Byt_IO prefixes to be omitted from the Get and Put procedure names.

Float_IO is the generic package in Text_IO for real numbers. The statement:

```
package Flt_IO is new Float_IO(Float);   use Flt_IO;
```

instantiates a package called Flt_IO with versions of Get and Put for variables and values of type Float.

The instantiation of packages is coded in the declaration section of a main procedure. A program that uses numeric IO has the structure:

```
with Text_IO;   use Text_IO;
procedure  program_name  is
    package Int_IO is new Integer_IO(Integer);   use Int_IO;
    package Flt_IO is new Float_IO(Float);    use Flt_IO;
    declarations - including data types, variables,
                   procedures and functions
begin
    statements
end program_name;
```

The Structure of Standard Input and Output

Standard input and output are text files. A text file is a collection of characters that may be organized into lines and pages using *line terminators*, and *page terminators*. The end of a file is indicated with a *file terminator*. We represent these terminators symbolically by:

<eoln>	for a line terminator
<eop>	for a page terminator
<eof>	for a file terminator

The example text file below contains three lines and one page; the second line is blank.

```
Star light, star bright <eoln>
<eoln>
first star I see tonight <eoln> <eop>
<eof>
```

While a text file is not required to have line and page terminators, a page terminator is always preceded by a line terminator.

Standard input and output are automatically opened when a program starts, and closed when a program ends. Input is read sequentially with the system keeping track of the current position and next available file component. The next component may be a character, or a line or page terminator.

Get and Put

As previously mentioned, the procedures Get and Put are used for reading and writing data, and a different Get and Put procedure is required for each data type. The term *overloading of procedure names* is used to express the concept of different procedures sharing a common name.

Data is read from input using a call to Get in the form:

```
Get(variable);
```

where "variable" stores the data "read." Get behaves differently depending on the data type of its argument.

With an argument of type Character:

Get reads the next file component that is a character, skipping over <eoln>s and <eop>s.

With an argument of type String:

Get reads successive character components, storing them in the string until the string is filled, skipping over <eoln>s and <eop>s.

With an argument of type Integer:

Get reads the next sequence of components representing an integer constant, skipping over blanks, <eoln>s and <eop>s.

With an argument of type Float:

Get reads the next sequence of components representing a real number or integer constant, skipping over blanks, <eoln>s, and <eop>s.

For Integer and Float data, Get converts the character representation of a number as a sequence of digits to the computer's internal representation of integers or floating-point-numbers. Also, Get does not skip over nonblank characters when reading values for Integer and Float variables, rather, a program error results and the default action is to abort the program.

Data is written to output using a call to Put in the form:

```
Put(value);
```

where "value" may be a variable or constant. Character and String data are written directly to output, whereas Integer and Float data are written using default formats. For example, the statement

```
Put(23.456)
```

might be output as

```
2.34560E+01
```

using an exponential notation as the default.

Put can take optional parameters specifying the format to use in writing Integer and Float data. The general form of Put for integers is

```
Put(value,width,base);
```

which causes "value" to be written right justified in a field of "width" characters, using the radix "base." Valid number bases are base 2 through 16. The general form of Put for real numbers is

```
Put(value,fore,aft,exp);
```

which causes "value" to be written with "fore" spaces allocated in front of the decimal point, "aft" spaces after the decimal point, and "exp" spaces allocated for a base 10 exponent. An "exp" value of 0 indicates not to use an exponential format. As an example, the statement

```
Put(23.456,2,2,0)
```

will generate the output

```
23.46
```

Additional IO Procedures and Functions

There are three Boolean functions to test for the current position in reading input: End_Of_Line, End_Of_Page, and End_Of_File.

End_Of_Line	returns True if the next component is <eoln> or <eof>; otherwise it returns False
End_Of_Page	returns True if the next two components are <eoln> <eop>, or the single component <eof>; otherwise it returns False
End_Of_File	returns True if the next component is either <eof> or the three-component sequence <eoln> <eop> <eof>; otherwise it returns False

The current position in the input file can be moved forward with the procedures Skip_Line and Skip_Page.

Skip_Line	moves the current position immediately past the next <eoln> component. If <eoln> is followed by <eop>, the current position is moved past <eop>. As a result, the next component can never be <eop>.
Skip_Page	moves the current position immediately past the next <eop> component.

Skip_Line can take an optional integer parameter to indicate the number of lines to skip past. So the call:

```
Skip_Line;
```

advances the current position one line, whereas,

```
Skip_Line(5);
```

advances the current position five lines.

New lines and pages can be started when writing to output with the procedures New_Line, New_Page, and Put_Line.

New_Line	causes the output of a line terminator, <eoln>, thus causing subsequent output to appear on a new line.
New_Page	causes the output of the two-component sequence <eoln> <eop>, thus marking the end of a page. If the last component output was a <eoln>, New_Page outputs only <eop>.
Put_Line	takes a string argument and outputs the string followed by <eoln>, thus terminating the current line.

New_Line can take an optional integer parameter to indicate the number of line terminators to output. So the call:

```
New_Line(5);
```

outputs five line terminators.

Examples:

Given the input file:

```
ABCD <eoln>
<eoln>
EFG<eoln>
<eof>
```

and Character variable Char, the code segment:

```
while (not End_Of_File) loop
    Get(Char);
    Put(Char);
end loop;
```

would produce as output:

```
ABCDEFG<eof>
```

whereas the code segment:

```
while (not End_Of_File) loop
    while (not End_Of_Line) loop
        Get(Char);
        Put(Char);
    end loop;
    Skip_Line;
    New_Line;
end loop;
```

would copy the input to output exactly.

As a further example, the following complete program reads integers one per line and prints their sum.

```
with Text_IO;  use Text_IO;
procedure Sum is
    package Int_IO is new Integer_IO(Integer);  use Int_IO;
    Value : Integer;
    Total : Integer := 0;
begin
    while (not End_Of_File) loop
        Get(Value);
        Skip_Line;
        Total := Value + Total;
    end loop;
    Put("The sum of the numbers is: ");
    Put(Total,8);
    New_Line;
end Sum;
```

2

FORMAL LANGUAGE DESCRIPTION

2.1 INTRODUCTION

The purpose of this chapter is to introduce the formalisms used to describe the syntactical structure of Ada. A simplified Backus-Naur-Form (BNF) is used, as appears in the *LRM*. Examples illustrate the correct syntax for language tokens such as integer and real number constants and the structure of a main procedure.

2.2 BNF NOTATION

There are three elements to a BNF description: terminals, nonterminals, and productions.

Terminals

Terminals are the symbols that may appear in an Ada source program. These are:

Uppercase and lowercase letters
ABCDEFGHIJKLMNOPQRSTUVWXYZ
abcdefghijklmnopqrstuvwxyz
Digits
0 1 2 3 4 5 6 7 8 9
The space character

Special characters
```
" # & ' ( ) * + , - . / : ; < = > _ |
! $ % ? @ [ \ ] ^ ' { } ~
```

These symbols are used to form syntactic units such as variable names (COUNT, Next_Item), numbers (-302, 14.25), and the assignment operator, ":=".

Nonterminals

Nonterminals represent syntactic units such as 'if_statement', 'integer_literal', and 'sequence_of_statements'. They will be represented in lowercase.

Productions

Productions are often called *rewrite rules*. They are rules for defining syntactic units in that they specify how to rewrite a syntactic unit in terms of other non-terminals and terminals. By "rewriting" nonterminals according to production rules until no nonterminals are present, valid Ada source code is derived. The notation for a production is:

N ::= S

where N is a nonterminal and S a sequence of terminals and/or nonterminals.

As an example, a production that defines the iteration structure commonly called a while loop (used in the sample program of Chapter 1) is:

```
loop_statement::= while condition loop
                     sequence_of_statements
                 end loop
```

Additional BNF notations

Productions are more concisely listed using the following standard conventional notations.

A vertical bar, |, represents alternative choices.
Square brackets, [ ], enclose an optional item.
Braces, { }, enclose zero or more repetitions of an item.

Using these symbols, an integer is described as:

digit ::= 0 | 1 | 2 | 3 | 4 | 5 | 6 | 7 | 8 | 9
integer ::= digit {[underline] digit}

Thus an integer is formed by a sequence of 1 or more digits with an optional underline between digits. Consecutive underlines are not allowed.

2.3 TOKENS

A token is a grouping of one or more terminals treated as a single entity within a program. There are five classes of tokens: delimiters, identifiers, numeric literals, character literals, and string literals.

Delimiters

Delimiters are often called *special symbols* and are used for a variety of purposes, including enclosing function arguments, representing arithmetic operators, and terminating statements.

Single character delimiters are:
> ( ) + - * / : ; , ' . | < > = &

Double character delimiters are:
> ** := <= >= /= => .. << >> <>

Identifiers

Identifiers are used as reserved words and as names of variables, procedures, etc. The production-defining identifiers are:

> identifier ::= letter { [underline] letter_or_digit }

This indicates that a valid identifier is a sequence of one or more alphanumeric characters that must start with a letter and which may contain the underline character. Consecutive underlines are not allowed. Identifiers are not case sensitive and may be of any length.

Examples

while	Old_Value	PL1	are valid identifiers.
COUNT	count	CoUnT	are the same identifier.
2nd_item	new__item		are invalid identifiers.

Numeric Literals

Ada provides several methods for writing numerical literals. Numbers can be expressed in base 2 through base 16, in addition to the usual base 10 representation. Thus, *based literals* are distinguished from *decimal literals*. In bases above 10, the letters *A* through *F* are used to represent the digits 10 through 15. The syntax for numeric literals is:

numeric_literal ::= decimal_literal | based_literal
decimal_literal ::= integer [. integer] [exponent]
integer ::= digit { [underline] digit }
exponent ::= E [+] integer | E - integer
based_literal ::=
        base # based_integer [. based_integer] # [exponent]
base ::= integer
based_integer ::=
        extended_digit { [underline] extended_digit }
extended_digit ::= digit | letter

Notice that underscores are allowed between digits in a number. This is for ease of reading and does not alter the value of the number. In addition, exponents are always powers of 10 and negative exponents are not allowed on integer constants.

Examples

34	23_602_345	10E+2	are integer literals.
3.1416	0.103	2.0E-3	are real literals.
2#1100#	5#22#	16# c#	are valid based literals; they all represent the same number.
_24	5E-2	.56	are invalid numeric constants.

Character Literals

A character literal is represented by enclosing the character within apostrophes. The syntax is:

character_literal ::= ' graphic_character '

Examples

'9'   '$'   'P'   ' '   '"'

String Literals

A string literal is represented by enclosing a sequence of zero or more characters within quotation marks. The syntax is:

string_literal ::= " { graphic_character } "

A single quotation mark is represented in a string literal by two adjacent quotation marks. The length of a string literal is the number of characters represented between the enclosing quotation marks.

Examples

""	is an empty string and has length 0
"A" "cat" """Hi"""	are strings of length 1, 3, and 4 respectively.

2.4 COMMENTS

In Ada source code, any line can contain a comment that, of course, is ignored by the compiler. A comment begins with a double hyphen "--" and extends to the end of the line. In a technical sense, a comment may not extend over more than one line. A lengthy comment is split into several comments on adjacent lines.

Example

```
--
--This is a long "comment" that must extend over
--several lines. Ada syntax requires that it be it
--split into several comments, one per line.
--
```

2.5 PROGRAM STRUCTURE

Compilation Units

Ada permits (indeed encourages) the modular design of programs by providing for the separate compilation of units of code. These *compilation units* may take several forms, from an individual procedure or function to *packages* of code that provide data types, procedures, and functions for use in other programs.

When compiled, these units are placed in a *program library*. A program indicates its intent to use a compilation unit through the use of a `with` clause. The sample program in Chapter 1 uses a compilation unit called `Text_IO`. This unit contains a package (also called `Text_IO`) that supplies the routines `Put`, `Get`, etc., for the input and output of character data.

Main Programs/Main Procedures

In Ada, any procedure or function that is a compilation unit has the potential of being used as a main program. However, an implementation of Ada is required only to permit parameterless procedures as main programs. The term *main procedure* is more appropriate than *main program*. The productions defining the syntax for a compilation unit consisting of a main procedure are:

```
compilation_unit  ::=  context_clause  library_unit
context_clause  ::=  {with_clause {use_clause}}
with_clause::=  with unit_name {, unit_name} ;
use_clause::=  use package_name {, package_name} ;
library_unit::=  subprogram_body
subprogram_body::=subprogram_specification  is
                    [declarative_part]
                begin
                        sequence_of_statements
                end  [identifier] ;
subprogram_specification::=  procedure identifier
sequence_of_statements::=  statement {statement}
```

Less formally, the standard format of an Ada main procedure is:

```
with units;  use packages;
procedure program_name is
    declarations -these include data types, variables,
                    procedures, and functions
begin
    sequence_of_statements
end  program_name;
```

Ada compilers place compiled units in a *program library*. They also provide methods for creating an executable file from a given compilation unit. This entails a phase during which program libraries (such as Text_IO) are linked with a main procedure or function.

3

SCALAR DATA TYPES/OPERATIONS/ EXPRESSIONS

3.1 INTRODUCTION

Ada provides a variety of data types for storing information. These types are indicated in Figure 3. 1. There are two kinds of scalar types: *discrete* and *real*. The discrete types are represented internally as integers and can be used as array indexes and for-loop parameters. There are two real-number types: floating and fixed point. Floating-point types have a constant number of significant digits, and hence are more dense when close to 0.0. Fixed-point types have a uniform density, successive numbers differing by a constant amount (which can be specified when they are declared).

This chapter discusses four scalar data types defined in the Ada package `Standard`. These are: `Integer`, `Float`, `Character`, and `Boolean`. Variables and constants storing these types of data are called *objects*. In addition, we will also cover universal and enumeration types. Arrays, records, and access (pointer) types are discussed in later chapters.

3.2 DECLARATIONS

The simplified syntax for declaring variables and constants having scalar data types is:

object_declaration ::=
        identifier_list : [**constant**] type [:= expression];

identifier_list ::= identifier [, identifier]

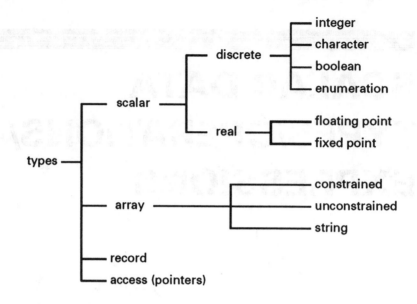

FIGURE 3.1 Ada Data Types

For this chapter, a type may be either `Integer`, `Float`, `Character`, `Boolean`, or an enumeration type.

Examples of declarations

```
TaxRate : Float := 0.12;
Count, Total : Integer := 0;
Start_Num: Integer := Total + 1;
Value: Integer;
Flag: Boolean;
Next_Char, Ch: Character;

DaysInWeek : constant := 7;   -- universal integer type
PI : constant  Float  := 3.1416;
YES, OK : constant Boolean := True;
```

Notice how variables can be given initial values when they are declared, although this is not required. The declaration of `Start_Num` illustrates how an intializer may be an expression that involves variables, as long as the variables have a value. A `constant` must have an initialization.

The declarative parts of a program require processing during the execution of the program. This processing includes such actions as allocating space for local variables within blocks, evaluating expressions used in initializing these variables, execcuting code to initialize packages, etc. In Ada, this is called the *elaboration* of the declarations. The term *elaboration* is used frequently in references to the Ada language. Keep in mind that declarations are elaborated during runtime, not during the program's compilation.

3.3 INTEGER AND FLOAT DATA

Unary Arithmetic Operations

Ada has three unary operations on numeric data:

Operation	Operator
absolute value	**abs**
unary plus	+
unary minus	-

The result of each operation has the same data type as the operand. Unary plus and minus are the usual identity and negation operations. It is noteworthy that absolute value is an operation, not a function as in many languages. A consequence of this is that **abs** does not have an argument, but rather an operand. Thus, for example, given an Integer variable Num with value -10, the expression:

```
abs  Num
```

without parentheses, is perfectly valid and has value +10. However, in the expression

```
abs  (-10)
```

the parentheses are required because there are two operations: absolute value and unary minus, and absolute value has the higher precedence.

Binary Arithmetic Operations

The binary operations on numeric data are:

Operation	Operator
exponentiation	**
multiplication	*
division	/
modulus	**mod**
remainder	**rem**
addition	+
subtraction	-

The left operand of exponentiation may be either `Float` or `Integer` data, and the result has this same type. The right operand must be an integer because exponentiation is defined as repeated multiplication, followed by taking a reciprocal if the exponent is negative. `Integer` data can have only nonnegative exponents.

Examples

5 ** 3	has value 125
5.0 ** 2	has value 125.0
5.0 ** (-2)	has value 0.04
5 ** (-2)	is an illegal expression
9.0 ** (0.5)	is an illegal expression

For multiplication, addition, and subtraction, both operands must have the same type, which in turn is the type of the result.

Examples

15 + 4	has value 19
15.2 + 4.0	has value 19.2
15.2 + 4	is an illegal expression

Division (/) is either real or integer division depending on the type of the operands. Integer division (divide and truncate) is done if the operands have type `Integer`; real division is done if the operands have type `Float`. Operands of different types are not allowed.

Examples

25 / 4	has value 6
-25 / 4	has value -6
25.0 / 4.0	Has value 6.25
25.0 / 4	is an illegal expression

Modulus (`mod`) and remainder (`rem`) are defined only for integer data; the result is also an integer. They are defined as:

A rem B = A - (A/B)*B

If B is positive, A mod B is the integer C, between 0 and B-1, inclusive such that (A - C) = nB, for some integer n.

If B is negative, then: A mod B = - ((-A) mod (-B)).

The difference between `rem` and `mod` is illustrated in Table 3.1.

A	B	A remB	A mod B
8	5	3	3
8	-5	3	-2
-8	-5	-3	-3
-8	5	-3	2

TABLE 3.1 Comparison of rem and mod

Type Conversions

The data type names `Integer` and `Float` can be used as function names to convert numeric values of one type to the other. `Float` values are rounded to the nearest integer when converted to `Integer`.

Examples:

Integer(2.4)	has value 2
Integer(2.5)	has value 3
Float(32/5)	has value 6.0

Because Ada is strongly typed, type conversions are necessary with expressions using data of differing numeric types. As an example, the code segment below reads an income (in whole dollars), and then calculates and prints a tax.

```
Income: Integer;  -- Stores Income in $
TaxRate: constant Float := 0.23;  -- 23 % Tax Rate
BaseTax: constant Float := 75.0;  -- Minimum Tax
TaxesOwed: Float;  -- Taxes owed
...
Get(Income);
TaxesOwed := BaseTax + Float(Income) * TaxRate;
Put('Taxes: ');
Put(TaxesOwed,5,2,0);
```

Relational Operators and Membership Tests

Numeric values of the same data type may be compared using the conventional relational operators. These are:

Operation	Operator
equality	=
inequality	/=
less	<
less/equal	<=

| greater | > |
| greater/equal | >= |

The results of these operations have a `Boolean` value of `True` or `False`. Used with the `Boolean` operations **and**, **or**, and **xor**, the relational operators are used to form conditional expressions in while loops, if statements, etc.

Membership test operators **in** and **not in** are used to determine if the value of an expression falls within a given range or subtype.

Examples

Given the `Integer` variable `Num`, the following code segment checks if `Num` has a value between 1 and 100:

```
if (Num in 1..100) then
     Put_Line("Num is between 1 and 100");
end if;
```

Given the subtype declaration:

```
subtype SmallNums is Integer range 1..100;
```

the condition above could be expressed as:

```
if (NUM in SmallNums) then
```

Operator Precedence

Operator precedence is given in the following table, from highest to lowest precedence.

highest precedence	** , abs, not
multiplying	*, /, mod, rem
unary adding	+, -
binary adding	+, -, &
relational/membership	=, /=, <, <=, >, >=, in, not in
logical	and, or, xor, and then, or else

As one would expect, parentheses can be used to alter the order in which operations are performed. In the absence of parentheses, operators at the same precedence level are evaluated from left to right.

Examples

| 2 + 3 * 5 | has value 17 |
| (2 + 3) * 5 | has value 30 |

45.0 / 2.0 * 3.0	has value 67.5
4 > 2 **and** 6 /= 13/2	has value False

Numeric Attributes

Ada defines the concept of an *attribute* for various entities in the language. An attribute is an operation that gives information about the entity. The Integer data type has two attributes: the smallest and largest possible integer values. These are denoted by:

Integer'First and Integer'Last

For a compiler that stores integers in 16-bit words, the value of Integer'First is -32768 and the value of Integer'Last is 32767.

The syntax for an attribute is:
attribute ::=
    prefix'attribute_designator [(universal_static_expression)]

Possible prefixes include types, variables, and procedure names. The permissible attribute_designators depend on the kind of entity the prefix is. Appendix I contains a list of attributes.

The attributes for the data type Float include:

Float'Digits	number of significant figures
Float'Small	smallest positive FLOAT number
Float'Large	largest positive FLOAT number

Of course, the values of these attributes depend on how a compiler represents floating-point numbers.

3.4 CHARACTER DATA

Character Constants

In Ada, the Character constants are those in the ASCII character set. These are enumerated in the package Standard. As mentioned in Chapter 2, character literals that have graphical representations are denoted between apostrophes, for example, 'A'. There is a package within Standard called ASCII which gives identifier names to all the characters, including those that do not have graphical representations. For example:

ASCII.LF	is a "line feed" (ascii code 10)
ASCII.NUL	is a "null" (ascii code 0)

ASCII.BEL	is the "bell" (ascii code 7)
ASCII.QUERY	is '?'
ASCII.LC_A	is 'a'

Operations and Attributes

The relational operators (=, /=, <, <=, >, >=) can be used to compare characters for ordering within the ASCII code. In addition, there are several useful attributes that operate as functions dealing with character data. Among these are:

Character'Succ	a function that takes a character argument and returns the next character in the ASCII collating sequence
Character'Pred	a function that takes a character argument and returns the preceding character in the ASCII collating sequence
Character'Pos	a function that takes a character argument and returns its integer ASCII code
Character'Val	a function that takes an integer argument and returns the character having this integer as its ASCII code

The following code segment reads a character from standard input and, if it is an uppercase letter, changes it to lowercase.

```
Get(Char);
if (Char in 'A'..'Z') then
    Char := Character'Val( Character'Pos(Char) + 32 );
end if;
```

3.5 BOOLEAN DATA

Boolean Literals

There are two literals of type `Boolean`: `False` and `True`.

Boolean Operations

As with any discrete data type, the relational operators (=, /=, <, etc.) can be used to compare Booleans for positional ordering (note: `False` is less than `True`). In addition, there are the usual Boolean operators: **and, or, xor, not.**

A	B	A and B	A or B	A xor B	not A
F	F	F	F	F	T
F	T	F	T	T	T
T	F	F	T	T	F
T	T	T	T	F	F

TABLE 3.2   Boolean Operators

These operators are defined in Table 3.2. When different Boolean operators are mixed in the same expression, parentheses are required for clarity. Thus the expression:

```
(i = j) or (k = 1) and (k = i)
```

is invalid and must be written:

```
((i = j) or (k = 1)) and (k = i)
```

When using the binary operators **and**, **or**, and **xor**, both operands are always evaluated. This is not always necessary; for example, in the expression:

```
(A > 0) and (A < 100)
```

if (A > 0) is False, the whole expression is False, so the second operand need not be evaluated. Skipping an unnecessary evaluation of an operand is called *short-circuit evaluation*. Ada provides explicit Boolean short-circuit operators: **and then** and **or else**. For these operators, the left operand is evaluated first and the right operand is not evaluated if the value of the whole expression can be determined from the left operand. This can lead to more straightforward code. As an example, consider the expression in the code segment below:

```
if (TestCount > 0) and (TestTotal/TestCount > 65) then
    Put_Line('Passing grade');
else
    Put_Line('Failing grade');
end if;
```

This code would cause a division by zero to be attempted if TestCount equals 0. To avoid this error, one could change the code to:

```
if (TestCount > 0) then
    if (TestTotal/TestCount > 65) then
        Put_Line('Passing Grade');
    else
        Put_Line('Failing Grade');
    end if;
else
    Put_Line('Failing Grade');
end if;
```

or, more concisely, use the **and then** operator:

```
if (TestCount > 0) and then (TestTotal/TestCount > 65) then
    Put_Line('Passing grade');
else
    Put_Line('Failing grade');
end if;
```

3.6 TYPES, SUBTYPES, AND UNIVERSAL TYPES

Type and Subtype Declarations

Ada permits the declaration of new numeric types and subtypes. Examples of declaration forms

```
type Days is range 1..31;
type Tax_Rate is digits 4 range 0.0..0.50;
type Int is new Integer;
type Symbols is new Character;

subtype Score is Integer range 0..100;
subtype Height is  Float range 0.05..120.4;
subtype UpCase is Character range 'A'..'Z';
```

Variables of these types can then be declared. The types Days, Tax_Rate, and Int are new numeric types that are not compatible with Integer or Float. As a result, a variable of type Days cannot be assigned to a variable of type Integer. These new types are said to be *derived* from Integer and Float. They have the standard arithmetic operations, and type conversions are allowed. On the other hand, Score is a **subtype** of Integer, so variables of these types are assignment compatible. Integer is said to be the *base type* of the subtype Score. In the examples above, Height has base type Float, and UpCase has base type Character.

When declaring new floating-point types, it is necessary to specify the precision with which the numbers are to be represented. The declaration of the data type Tax_Rate indicates that variables of this type are to be represented with four decimal places of precision.

Universal Types

In Ada, integer literals have the type *universal_integer*. Real-number literals have type *universal_real*. These universal types are compatible with all integer and floating-point types respectively. This permits literals to be used with all types of numeric data.

Example declarations

```
type Age is range 0..120;

My_Age   : Age;
Your_Age : Integer;
```

Because the literal 27 has type *universal_integer*, the assignments:

```
My_Age := 27;
Your_Age := 27;
```

are both valid. If 27 had type `Integer`, the assignment to the variable `My_Age` would be invalid because of a type mismatch.

Constants having a universal type are declared by omitting an explicit type identifier. For example:

```
FaradayConst : constant := 96_500;     -- coul/mole
AvagadroNum  : constant := 6.025E+23;  -- molecules/mole
```

3.7 ENUMERATION TYPES

An enumeration type is a discrete type whose literals are specified at the time of declaration. Simplified syntax for an enumeration type definition is:

enumeration_type_definition ::=
    (enumeration_literal,{, enumeration_literal})
enumeration_literal ::= identifier | character_literal

Examples

```
type Colors is (red, white, blue);
type Days is (Mon,Tue,Wed,Thu,Fri,Sat,Sun);
type Vowels is ('a','e','i','o','u');
subtype WeekEnd is Days range Sat..Sun;
```

Notice that character literals can be used as enumeration literals. When used in this way, they are not compatible with `Character` data. In the example above, the type `Vowels` is not even a subtype of the type `Character`.

The literals of an enumeration type are ordered by the position in which they are listed. The first literal has position 0, the second has position 1, the third position 2, and so on. For example, as a `Vowels` literal, `'a'` has position 0; as a `Character`, literal `'a'` has position 97.

Enumeration variables can be declared, assigned values, and compared. Attributes of enumeration types include `First`, `Last`, `Succ`, `Pred`, `Pos`, `Val` (see Appendix I.) These attributes are similar to those for character data. `Text_IO` contains a generic package called `Enumeration_IO`, which can be instantiated to provide IO routines for enumeration types.

Example program

```
with Text_IO; use Text_IO;
procedure Enums is
    -- Print the position values of an enumeration type.
        type Days is (Mon,Tue,Wed,Thu,Fri,Sat,Sun);
        package Days_IO is new Enumeration_IO(Days);
        package Int_IO is new Integer_IO(Integer);
        use Days_IO, Int_IO;
        Today : Days;
begin
Today := Mon;
loop
        Put(Today);               -- Write current day.
        Put(Days'Pos(Today),5);   -- Write its position.
        New_Line;
        exit when (Today = Days'Last); -- Exit loop if Sun.
        Today := Days'Succ(Today);     -- Go to next day.
    end loop;
    end Enums;
```

4

STATEMENTS

4.1 INTRODUCTION

In Ada, the term *statement* refers to a program construct defining an action to be performed. The action is performed when the statement is *executed*. Two types of statements are distinguished: *simple* and *compound*. Compound statements surround other statements, whereas simple statements do not. Examples of simple statements are assignment, procedure calls, and the goto statement. Compound statements include loop, if, and case. (For a complete list, see the syntax diagrams for *simple_statement* and *compound_statement* in Appendix K.)

The more common simple and compound statements are discussed in this chapter. These include assignment and the control statements for implementing selection (if and case) and repetition (loops). Other statements are covered in later chapters in the context of their use.

It is worthwhile to note that in Ada, the semicolon, ";", terminates and is considered part of each statement. The syntax for a sequence of statements is:

sequence_of_statements ::= statement {statement}

Notice that there must be at least one statement and that the semicolon is not shown in the "rewrite rule." The semicolon appears, as you will see, in the rule defining each statement.

4.2 ASSIGNMENT STATEMENT

The assignment operator in Ada is the delimiter ":=". The syntax for an assignment statement is:

assignment_statement ::= variable_name := expression;

The left side of the statement must name a variable; the right side is an expression having a type compatible with the variable on the left. When the statement executes, the expression on the right of the ":=" is evaluated, and its value is assigned to the variable whose name is on the left.

Examples

```
Count := Count + 1;
Char  := 'A';
Flag  := (Char /= 'B');    -- Flag is a Boolean variable
```

4.3 THE NULL STATEMENT

Because every sequence of statements in Ada must contain at least one statement, it is convenient to have a statement that does nothing, that is, performs no action. The **null** statement fills this role. Its syntax is:

null_statement ::= **null**;

Like all statements, the null statement is terminated with a semicolon. An example of its use is shown in section 4.5 on the **case** statement.

4.4 THE BLOCK STATEMENT

A **block** statement encapsulates a collection of declarations and statements into a unit for the purpose of restricting the scope of identifiers and handling exceptions occurring within the unit.
    Simplified syntax for the **block** statement is:

block_statement ::=
    [block_name :]
        [**declare**
            declarative_part]
        begin
            sequence_of_statements
        [**exception**
            exception_handler
            { exception_handler }]
        end [block_name];

The only required structure is to bracket the sequence of statements with **begin end**; even declarations of variables local to the block are optional. Exception handlers can be present and their use in block statements is discussed in detail in Chapter 12. The block statement below interchanges the values of integer variables named Num_1 and Num_2.

```
declare
    Temp : Integer := Num_1;
begin
    Num_1 := Num_2;
    Num_2 := Temp;
end;
```

The variable Temp is not needed outside of the block and may be referenced only within the block. The declarative part in this example is quite simple, but in general may contain any declarative item, including types, subtypes, subprograms, and packages.

4.5 SELECTION STATEMENTS

Selection statements permit one group of statements to be chosen for execution to the exclusion of others. Ada has two control structures for implementing selection: the if_statement and the case_statement.

If Statement

The syntax of the if statement is:

```
if_statement::=if condition then
                   sequence_of_statements
               {elsif condition then
                   sequence_of_statements }
               [else
                   sequence_of_statements ]
               end if;
```

The initial **if** clause may be followed by zero or more **elsif** clauses and an optional **else** clause. The conditions are evaluated in sequence. As soon as one condition evaluates to True, the corresponding sequence_of_statements is executed. Subsequent conditions are not evaluated; execution continues with any statements following the **end if**. If all the conditions evaluate to False, the statements in an optional **else** clause will be executed.

Example:

```
if (Score in 0..100) then
    -- Calculate a letter grade.
    if (Score >= 90) then
```

```
      Grade := 'A';
   elsif (Score >= 80) then
      Grade := 'B;
   elsif (Score >= 70) then
      Grade := 'C';
   elsif (Score >= 60) then
      Grade := 'D';
   else
      Grade := 'F';
   end if;
   Put('The letter grade is: ');
   Put(Grade);
   New_Line;
end if;
```

Case Statement

A case statement selects one out of several statement sequences to execute on the basis of the value of an expression.

The syntax of the case statement is:

> case_statement ::=
>   **case** expression **is**
>   **when** choice { | choice } => sequence_of_statements
>   { **when** choice { | choice } => sequence_of_statements }
>   **end case;**

where

> choice ::= simple_expression | discrete_range |
>   **others** | component_simple_name

An example of a case statement, which produces the same result as the if statement in the last section is:

```
case Score is
    when  90..100=>  Grade := 'A';
    when  80..89=>  Grade := 'B';
    when  70..79=>  Grade := 'C';
    when  60..69=>  Grade := 'D';
    when   0..59=>  Grade := 'F';
    when others=>  null;
end case;
```

The semantics of the case statement is that the expression is evaluated and its value matched with a choice. The statement sequence following the choice is then executed. If present, an **others** choice must appear last and is taken by default when the previous choices fail to match the expression.

The choices must be disjoint and every possible value that the expression may assume must be represented in the choices. So, although an **others** choice is not required, it is often used.

Here is one additional `case` example:

```
case Grade is
    when 'A' | 'B' | 'C' | 'D'  =>  Put_Line('passing grade');
    when 'F' =>  Put_Line('failing grade');
    when others=>  Put_Line('error - invalid grade');
end case;
```

4.6 LOOP STATEMENTS

Loop statements permit the repetition of a statement sequence. Ada has three constructs for expressing repetition: `while`, `loop`, and `for` statements. A simplified description of the syntax of the loop constructs is:

> loop_statement ::=[iteration scheme] **loop**
> > > sequence_of_statements
> > **end loop;**

where

> iteration_scheme ::=**while** condition |
> > > **for** loop_parameter_specification

Notice that the iteration scheme is optional.

The Loop Statement

A loop statement with no iteration scheme has the form:

> **loop**
> > sequence_of_statements
> **end loop;**

In structure, this is an infinite loop. One common way to terminate such a loop is with an `exit` statement, as in the following example, which prints a list of the first 10 integers.

```
Count := 0;
loop
    Count := Count + 1;
    Put(Count,3);
    New_Line;
    exit when (Count = 10);
end loop;
```

The `exit` statement is described in detail in section 4.7. It may appear any number of times in a loop statement to test for varying termination conditions. The following code segment reads characters from standard input until either the end of the file is reached or a '!' is encountered.

```
loop
        exit when End_Of_File;
        Get(Char);
        exit when (Char = '!');
end loop;
```

The While Iteration Scheme

Technically speaking, Ada does not have a "while statement," but rather a loop statement with a "while iteration scheme." The general format is:

while condition **loop**
    sequence_of_statements
end loop;

The condition must be an expression having a `Boolean` value, and is evaluated prior to the execution of the statement sequence within the loop. If the condition is `True`, the statement sequence is executed. This process is repeated until the condition evaluates to `False`. Execution then continues with any statements following the loop. Examples of using **while** that have the same results as the previous loop examples are:

```
Count := 0;
while (Count /= 10) loop
    Count := Count + 1;
    Put(Count,3);
    New_Line;
end loop;
```

and

```
Char := ' ';-- initialize char to a blank
while (not End_Of_File) and (Char /= '!') loop
    Get(Char);
end loop;
```

The For Iteration Scheme

The syntax for the **for** iteration scheme is:

for loop_parameter_specification

where:

loop_parameter_specification ::=
                    identifier **in** [**reverse**] discrete_range

Less formally, the structure of this type of loop is:

for identifier **in** [**reverse**] discrete_range **loop**
    sequence_of_statements
end loop;

A loop that prints the first 10 integers is:

```
for Count in 1..10 loop
    Put(Count,3);
    New_Line;
end loop;
```

Additional examples of **for** iteration schemes are:

```
for i in 1..(N+1) loop
for Char in reverse 'a'..'z' loop
for Char in Character loop
for Count in (Value*2)..(X+5) loop
```

The identifier, often called the *loop parameter* or *loop control variable*, must not be declared as a program variable. It is implicitly declared by its use in the loop construct, and its scope is restricted to the loop construct. Thus it redefines any identifier of the same name within its scope.

As indicated in the examples, the discrete_range over which the loop parameter ranges may be specified using constants or expressions, or by a discrete data type identifier. The loop identifier is implicitly declared to be of the appropriate type. Ordinarily the loop parameter is initialized to the starting value of the range and advanced to its successor at each iteration of the loop. If the **reverse** option is included, the loop parameter is initialized to the ending value of the range and decreased to its predecessor at each iteration. When the loop parameter is advancing, the sequence_of_statements is executed only if the parameter's value is less than or equal to the ending range value. Thus it is possible that the loop statements are never executed. Similar remarks apply if the **reverse** option is used.

Here are some additional examples of the use of the **for** iteration scheme.

Examples

```
-- Find the cardinality of the discrete data type Character.

    Number := 0;
    for Char in Character loop
        Number := Number + 1;
    end loop;
    Put("There are ");
    Put(Number);
    Put_Line(" data items in the Character data type.");

-- Print the first 10 integers in reverse order

    for i in reverse 1..10 loop
        Put(i,3);
        New_Line;
    end loop;
```

4.7 TRANSFER STATEMENTS

The Exit Statement

An **exit** statement is used to terminate a loop. There are both conditional and unconditional forms of the statement. The syntax is:

exit_statement ::= **exit** [**when** condition];

When an exit statement is executed, program control is transferred to the statement after the closest enclosing loop. A loop can contain several exit statements to reflect different reasons for exiting the loop. If the **when** option is used, the `exit` statement is executed only if the condition evaluates to True.

As an example, the program segment below reads and builds an integer from a line of input, printing an error message if nondigit characters are encountered.

```
Sign    := 1;
Number := 0;
Get(Char);
if (Char = '-') then
    Sign := -1;
    Get(Char);
end if;
loop
    if (Char not in '0'..'9') then
        Put_Line("error - bad char in number");
        exit;
    end if;
    Number := Number * 10 +
            Character'Pos(Char) - Character'Pos('0');
    exit when (End_Of_Line);
    Get(Char);
end loop;
```

The Goto Statement

The `goto` statement is used to permit unconditional transfer of control to a labeled target statement. In effect, it allows a jump from one part of a program to another in an unstructured manner. Current programming convention discourages using the `goto` because it can result in poor program design. Nevertheless it is among the oldest control structures and is still provided by many programming languages, including Ada. The syntax of the `goto` statement is:

goto_statement ::= **goto** label_name;
label_name ::= << identifier >>

Note that the label on the target statement is simply an identifier enclosed within << >> symbols. A degenerate example of a **goto**'s use is:

```
<<front>>      Put ("I'm caught   ");
               goto  middle;
<<rear>>       Put_Line ("loop!");
               goto  front;
<<middle>>     Put ("in an infinite ");
               goto  rear;
```

The use of the goto statement is restricted. A goto cannot be used to jump from the outside to the inside of constructs such as loop, if, case, and block statements. It is prohibited to jump from the "then clause" to the "else clause" of an if statement, between the alternative parts of a case statement, or out of a program block such as a procedure or function.

In general, the **goto** allows for a jump within a statement sequence (as in the example above) or to the outside of an enclosing control structure. Here is another example:

```
<<get_response>>Put ("continue the program (y/n)? ");
                Get (Key_Pressed);
                Skip_Line;
                if (Key_Pressed /= 'y')
                        and
                   (Key_Pressed /= 'n') then
                      Put_Line ("invalid response");
                      goto get_response;
                end if;
```

Other Transfer Statements

Several additional statements can be used to control the flow of a program. These include statements to **raise** exceptions, **terminate** or **abort** tasks, and **return** from procedures or functions. Discussion of each of these is deferred to later chapters so that they can be viewed in the appropriate context.

5
STRUCTURED DATA TYPES

5.1 INTRODUCTION

There are two common data types for building composite structures with several components: arrays and records. Ada has a variety of kinds of arrays and records (including strings and variant records), providing a rich environment for designing data structures.

5.2 ARRAYS

An array is a data structure consisting of a linear sequence of components of the same data type. The location of each component is specified by an index, with the set of indexes chosen from a discrete range of values. The number of values in the range determines the number of components, or elements, in the array.

In Ada, array types can be defined and then variables of this type can be declared. Alternatively, array variables can be declared directly, without an explicit type declaration. Ada has both constrained and unconstrained arrays. *Constrained arrays* have a fixed number of components with a fixed index range. *Unconstrained arrays* may have a variable number of components indexed by different ranges from a given discrete type.

Constrained Array Declarations

The syntax for declaring constrained arrays is:

    constrained_array_definition ::=
            array index_constraint **of** component_subtype_indication

where

> index_constraint ::= (discrete_range { , discrete_range })

Example type declarations

```
type List is array(1..5) of Integer;
type Flags is array(Character) of Boolean;
type Decade is array(1990..1999) of Float;
type Two_D is array(1..4,1..6) of Float;
type Three_D is array(-2..7,'A'..'Z',1..4) of Character;
```

Array objects (variables) can then be declared:

```
Vector : List;
Matrix : Two_D;
```

One can also declare array objects directly, as in:

```
Vector : array(1..5) of Integer;
Matrix : array(1..4,1..6) of Float;
```

Assignments and Initializations

A single array component is referenced with an index enclosed within parentheses after the array name. Thus the statements:

```
Vector(4) := 15;
Matrix(2,3) := 4.7;
```

assign values to individual elements in the arrays vector and matrix. Assignments are also permitted between arrays of the same type and between array slices. An *array slice* is a portion of an array and is referenced by an index range (as opposed to a single index value). The syntax for a slice is:

> slice ::= prefix(discrete range)

where the prefix is the name of an array. Examples of array slices are:

```
Vector(1..3)  -- The front portion of the array Vector
Name(1..Length)  -- From the sample program of Chapter 1.
```

Example assignments involving arrays

Given the declarations:

```
type Line is array(1..80) of Character;
A, B : Line;
```

The following assignments are valid:

```
A(4) := B(7);-- Assignment between single elements.
A := B;      -- Assignment between whole arrays.
```

```
A(30..39) := B(50..59);-- Assignment between 10
                       --  element slices.
```

Assignments can also be made using **array aggregates** such as:

```
Vector := (23,-4,6,10,8);   -- Initialize the array vector.
A := (1..80 => ' ');        -- Initialize A to blanks.
A := (1..40 => 'A', others => ' '); -- Set first 40 characters
                                    -- in A to 'A's, and the
                                    -- rest to blanks.
```

An *aggregate* is an operation for combining components of an array (or record) into the composite structure. The examples above illustrate the two methods of specifying aggregates: *positional* and *named*. The positional form is used to initialize Vector. Each value is matched implicitly to its corresponding array component by its position in the aggregate. The array A is initialized using the named form, in which the component being initialized is named (in this case by its index). Positional and named forms can be combined, but the positional form must appear first. The choice **others** is optional, must appear last, and refers to all remaining components.

The following assignments to Vector are equivalent.

```
Vector := (23,-4,6,10,8);
Vector := (23, -4, 4 => 10, 5 => 8, 3 => 6);
```

Initializations with aggregates can be made at the time the array objects are declared, for example:

```
A : Line := (1..80 => ' ');
```

As an additional example, the following three code segments all set A to blanks:

```
for i in 1..80 loop
    A(i) := ' ';
end loop;
for i in 1..40 loop
    A(2*i-1..2*i) := (' ',' ');
end loop;
A := (1..80 => ' ');
```

Array Attributes

Arrays have several useful attributes. Let List be an array object, or a constrained array type, then the following attributes are defined:

List'First	the lower bound of the first index range.
List'Last	the upper bound of the first index range.
List'Range	the range List'First..List'Last.

List'Length	the number of values in the first index range.
List'First(n)	the lower bound of the nth index range.
List'Last(n)	the upper bound of the nth index range.
List'Range(n)	the range List'First(n)..List'Last(n).
List'Length(n)	the number of values in the nth index range.

Example

For the array types and objects declared previously we have:

List'First	is 1.
Decade'Range	is 1990..1999.
Three_D'Last(2)	is 'Z'.
Matrix'Last(1)	is 4.

Unconstrained Arrays

An *unconstrained array* is one for which the number of components is specified at the time of the array object declaration. The array type definition contains only a specification of the index type and component type. The syntax for the array definition is:

unconstrained_array_definition ::=
       array (index_subtype_definition {, index_subtype_definition})
                      of component_subtype_indication

where

index_subtype_definition ::= type_mark **range** <>

Example type declarations

```
type Year_Sales is array (Integer range <>) of  Float;
type Char_Count is array (Character range <>) of Integer;
type Grid is array(Integer range <>,Integer range <>) of Integer;
```

Notice that only the index range type is specified, not the number of components, nor the specific range of index values. These are specified when the array objects are declared, and may be different for array objects of the same unconstrained type. For example:

```
List_For_90s      : Year_Sales(1990..1999);
List_For_Century  : Year_Sales(1900..1999);
Square_Matrix     : Grid(1..10,1..10);
Matrix            : Grid(1..4,1..20);
```

Unconstrained arrays are particularly useful for writing general procedures and functions. The function below uses array attributes and returns the sum of the elements in an array of type Year_Sales. Note the use of array attributes to specify the first and last subscripts of the array. This enables the function to operate correctly for arrays of different lengths.

```
function TotalSales(SalesList : in Year_Sales) return Float is
    -- Return the sum of the elements in the array SalesList.
    Total : Float := 0.0;    -- Initialize the total to zero.
begin
for i in SalesList'First..SalesList'Last loop
    Total := Total + SalesList(i);
end loop;
return (Total);
end TotalSales;
```

Note that the **for** *loop_parameter_specification* in the function above could have been written as:

```
for i in SalesList'Range loop
```

5.3 STRINGS

Character strings are implemented in Ada with the predefined type String, an unconstrained array.

```
subtype Positive is Integer range 1..Integer'Last;
type String is array(Positive range <>) of Character
```

Example String object declarations

```
FileName : String(1..20);
ErrMsg   : constant String := "error - file not found";
Line     : String(1..80);
```

Strings and string slices can be compared using lexicographic order with the operators =, <, <=, >, >=, and /=. Comparisons are permitted between strings of different lengths. Uppercase and lowercase letters are considered different. In addition, strings can be concatenated using the operator &.

Ada does not have variable length strings, necessitating extensive use of array slices. As an example, code to read a name and print a greeting is shown below. The input procedure Get_Line, supplied by Text_IO, is used.

```
Put("Please type your name: ");
Get_Line(Line,Length);
Line(1..Length+6) := "Hello " & Line(1..length)
Put(Line(1..Length+6)); New_Line;
```

5.4 RECORDS

A record is a data structure consisting of a collection of components of (possibly) different data types. The components are called the *fields* of the record and are referenced by an identifier name (as opposed to being referenced by an index, as for arrays). As a general rule, one thinks of objects of the same record type as having the same component structure. While this is often the case, Ada also permits record variants in which record objects of the same type can have different sets of components based upon the value of one component, called the *discriminant*. Records with a fixed structure are considered first in this chapter, followed by records with discriminants.

Record Declarations and Assignments

Simplified syntax for declaring a record type is:

        record_type_definition ::= **record**

                                        component_list
                                end record

where

        component_list ::=
                component_declaration { component_declaration } |
                { component_declaration } variant part |
                null;

and

        component_declaration ::=
                        identifier_list : type [:= expression];

Records with a variant part are covered in a later section.

Example type declarations (without variant part)

```
type DigitString is array(1..9) of Character range '0'..'9';
type PartInfo is
    record
        PartNumber: DigitString;
        Description: String(1..50);
        Price : Float;
        InStock: Integer := 0;
    end record;

type DayInfo is
    record
        Month: Integer range 1..12;
```

```
            Day: Integer range 1..31;
            Year: Integer range 0..3000;
        end record;

type EmployeeData is
        record
            Name: String(1..20);
            BirthDate: DayInfo;
            Address: String(1..30);
        end record;
```

Example variable declarations

```
Part1, Part2: PartInfo;
EmployeeList: array(1..200) of EmployeeData;
Manager: EmployeeData;
```

Notice that records can have components that are arrays and even other records. Also, arrays of records can be declared.

Components of a record can be given default values by initializers. In the examples above, the InStock field of the variables Part1 and Part2 are automatically initialized to 0.

A record object may be referenced by its name for the purpose of comparision or assignment.

Examples

```
Part1 := Part2;
Employee(3) := Manager;
if (Employee(i) = Employee(i+1)) then
    Duplicate := True;
end if;
```

The individual components of a record are referenced by the record name, followed by a period, followed by the component name. This is called a *selected_component* and has the syntax:

selected_component ::= prefix.selector

where the prefix is the name of a record object and the selector is the field name of the component being referenced.

Examples

```
Part1.PartNumber:= "000045005";
Part2.PartNumber(4):= '5';
EmployeeList(3).Name:= "John Doe              ";
Manager.BirthDate.Month:= 9;
```

It is also possible to make an assignment to all the fields of a record, using either positional or named aggregates.

Example (using a positional aggregate)

```
Part1 := ("000045005",43.50,230);
```

Records with Discriminants

A *discriminant* is a parameter to a record declaration that can be used to specify alternative logical forms of the record. It is a component of the record, must have a discrete data type, and may be given a default value. A discriminant can be used in a record to specify an initial value for a field, the index range of an array, a variant record form, or the value of a discriminant for a field.

The syntax of a full type definition for a record with discriminant is:

full_type_definition ::=

      type identifier [discriminant_part] **is**

            record

                component_list

            end record;

where

discriminant_part ::=

  (discriminant_specification {; discriminant_specification})

discriminant_specification ::=

      identifier_list : type [:= expression]

Examples

```
-- Using discriminants to define initial field values.

type CreditLine (Limit : Integer) is
        record
              Ceiling : Integer := Limit;   -- Initial value.
              Balance : Float := 0;
        end record;

type Days is (Mon,Tue,Wed,Thu,Fri,Sat,Sun);
type Meeting (Hour: Integer := 1300; Day: Days := Fri) is
        record
              M_time  : Integer := Hour;
              M_day   : Days := Day;
              M_place : String(1..30);
        end record;
```

```
     -- Using discriminants to define index ranges of arrays

type Buffer (Size : Integer := 80) is
     record
          Contents : String(1..Size);
          Location : Integer := 0;
       end record;
type Matrix is
     array(Integer range <>, integer range <>) of Float;
type SqMatrix (n : Integer) is
          record
                Mat : Matrix(1..n,1..n);
          end record;
```

Notice that types `Meeting` and `Buffer` have default discriminant values. Default values must be given to either all or none of the discriminants of a type. When declaring variables, the value of the discriminant is specified in parentheses, after the type name. This is called a *discriminant constraint*, and is required if there is no default value. If discriminants are not constrained, default values are used.

Examples

```
NewAcct   : CreditLine(2000);      -- $2000 initial credit ceiling.
Interview : Meeting;               -- Meet on Fri at 1300 hours.
Lunch     : Meeting(1200,Wed);     -- Lunch at noon on Wed.
Line      : Buffer;                -- An 80-character buffer.
ShortLine : Buffer(40);            -- A 40-character buffer.
LongLine  : Buffer(256);           -- A 256-character buffer.
Grid      : SqMatrix(5);           -- A 5x5 square matrix.

Acct : CreditLine;   -- Error! discriminant constraint required.
A : SqMatrix;        -- Error! discriminant constraint required.
```

Issues Involving Discriminant Constraints

A discriminant constraint defines a subtype of the original record type. Thus (using the previous examples) `Buffer(40)` is a subtype of `Buffer`. It could be explicitly declared:

```
subtype SmallBuffer is Buffer(40);
```

It is illegal to change the value of the discriminant of an object declared with a discriminant constraint. The discriminant value fixes the form of the record. Given the declarations:

```
ShortLine : Buffer(40);     -- A constrained object.
Line      : Buffer;         -- An unconstrained object.
```

the variable `ShortLine` is a 40-character buffer whose size cannot be altered, while `Line` has an initial size of 80, but may be changed by altering the value of the discriminant.

The value of a discriminant cannot be changed directly, but only if the entire record is assigned new values using a record aggregate. For example, the variable `Line` is initially an 80-character buffer, and while the statements:

```
Line.Size := 256;    -- Illegal statement.
Line.contents := (1..256 => ' ');
Line.location := 0;
```

do not change it to a 256-character buffer, the following statement does:

```
Line := (256, (1..256 => ' '), 0);
```

Variant Records

A *variant record* is a record that can have more than one logical form. The logical form that the record assumes is determined by the value of a *discriminant*. The syntax of a record definition with a variant part is:

> record_type_definition ::=
>
> > **record**
> >
> > > { component_declaration }
> > > variant_part
> >
> > **end record**

where

> variant_part ::=
>
> > **case** discriminant_simple_name **is**
> >
> > > variant
> > > {variant }
> >
> > **end case;**

> variant ::= **when** choice { | choice } => component_list

> choice ::=simple_expression | discrete_range |
> > **others** | component_simple_name

Examples

```
type Transportation is (Auto, Truck, Bus);
type Vehicle (Kind : Transportation := Auto) is
            record
                EngineSize : Float;    -- In cubic inches.
                case Kind is
                    when Auto =>
                        AirCond     : Boolean;
```

```
                           AutoTrans  : Boolean;
                           GasMileage : Float;
                    when Truck =>
                           Tons  : Float;
                           Axles : Integer;
                    when Bus =>
                           Capacity : Integer;
                           ModelYr  : Integer;
              end record;

type EmployeeInfo (PayType : Integer) is
              record
                   Name    : String(1..30);
                   Address : String(1..40);
                    case PayType is
                       when 1 | 2 | 3 =>    -- Hourly wage.
                          Wages : Float;
                          Hours : Float;
                          OTime : Float;
                       when 4..10 =>    -- Commissioned.
                          Rate  : Float;
                          Sales : Float;
                       when 11 =>    -- Salaried.
                          Salary : Float;
                       when others =>
                          null;
              end record;
```

The type `EmployeeInfo` illustrates that alternative values of the discriminant can select the same record variant. These values can be listed, separated by the symbol "|", or they may be indicated by a discrete range. Each value of the discriminant type must appear once and only once in the set of choices. An exception is the choice **others**, which stands for all values not appearing in the previous choices. An **others** choice is not required but, when present, must be on the last variant.

Example variable declarations

```
Transport : Vehicle;         -- Unconstrained, 'auto' by default.
Tanker : Vehicle(Truck);     -- Constrained to 'truck' vehicle.
Empl_1 : EmployeeInfo(1);    -- Works for wages.
Empl_2 : EmployeeInfo(7);    -- Works on commission.
Empl_3 : EmployeeInfo(11);   -- A salaried employee.
Empl_4 : EmployeeInfo; -- Illegal,
                       -- discriminant must be constrained.
```

`Transport` and `Tanker` are variants of the same base type, `Vehicle`. Their structure is illustrated in Figure 5.1. As noted previously, the structure of a constrained record (such as `Tanker`, or `Empl_1`) cannot be changed. The structure of an unconstrained record can be altered through the assignment of an appropriate record aggregate. For example:

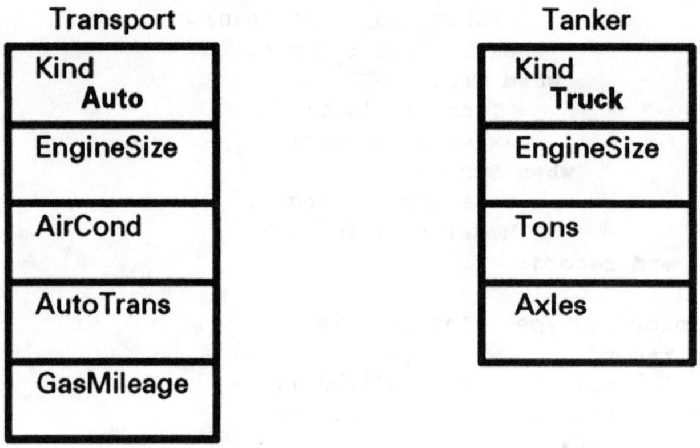

Transport

| Kind **Auto** |
| EngineSize |
| AirCond |
| AutoTrans |
| GasMileage |

Tanker

| Kind **Truck** |
| EngineSize |
| Tons |
| Axles |

FIGURE 5.1 Structure of variant records

```
Transport := (Truck,350,2,2);
```

or

```
Transport := (Kind => Bus, EngineSize => 300,
              Capacity => 60, ModelYr => 1991);
```

6 PROCEDURES AND FUNCTIONS

6.1 INTRODUCTION

Procedures and functions are the fundamental tools for designing and building modular programs. Both are invoked by their names and may be passed parameters. The difference is that procedures are used to execute a group of statements, whereas functions are used to determine and return a value that is used in an expression. Ada allows these subprograms to be used in a variety of ways. They can be nested within main procedures or other subprograms, compiled separately and linked with any program that needs them, or grouped with other routines to provide a package of related services. Indeed, standard packages of subprograms (such as `Text_IO`) are provided with every Ada compilation system. This chapter shows how to declare and use procedures and functions.

6.2 PROCEDURES

Declaration/Body

A distinction is made between a procedure declaration and a procedure body. Simplified syntax for a procedure declaration is:

    subprogram_declaration ::= subprogram_specification;
    subprogram_specification ::=
                        procedure identifier [formal_part]

where

[formal_part] ::=

        (parameter_specification {; parameter_specification})

parameter_specification ::=

        identifier_list : mode type [:= expression]

mode ::= [in] | **in out** | **out**

Examples

```
procedure Swap(a, b : in out Integer);
procedure Sort(List : in out ArrayType; Size : in Integer);
procedure Skip_Three_Lines;
```

The primary use of declarations is to permit a procedure name and parameter requirements to be available to other compilation units separate from the procedure body, which contains the executable statements. Another use is for what is known as a *forward declaration*. A forward declaration is needed for a procedure that is called by a subprogram preceding it in the source code. Placing the declaration before both routines allows a compiler to generate the correct code for the procedure call.

Simplified syntax for a procedure body is:

subprogram_body ::= **procedure** identifier [formal_part] **is**
                [declarative_part]
        begin
            sequence_of_statements
        end identifier;

Examples:

A **procedure** declaration:

```
procedure Swap(a,b: in out Integer);
```

A **procedure** body:

```
procedure Swap(a,b: in out Integer) is
              -- Interchange the values of a and b.
     Temp : Integer := a;   -- Temp helps in the swap.
begin
a := b;
b := Temp;
end Swap;
```

Another example of a procedure body is shown below. The procedure sorts an array and contains a call to the swap procedure.

```
procedure Sort(List: in out ArrayType; Size: in Integer) is
        -- Sort the Integer array list, use Selection Sort.
    Min : Integer;  -- Index of smallest unsorted element.
begin
for i in 1..(Size-1) loop           -- Locate the smallest
    Min := i;                       -- element in the index
    for j in (i+1)..Size loop           -- range i..Size
        if (List(j) < List(Min)) then   -- and swap it with
            Min := j;                   -- the ith element.
        end if;
    end loop;
    Swap(List(i),List(Min));
end loop;
end Sort;
```

Procedure Calls

A procedure is invoked by its name in a procedure call statement. The syntax is:

procedure_call_statement ::=
            procedure_name [actual_parameter_part];

where

actual_parameter_part ::=
            (parameter_association {, parameter_association})
parameter_association ::=
            [formal_parameter =>] actual_parameter

Notice that parameters are optional, but if present are listed within parentheses and separated by commas. Parameters may be specified in two ways: *positional* and *named*.

In *positional* association, the actual parameters are in one-to-correspondence with the formal parameters. As an example, the procedure Sort, in the previous section, makes a call to the procedure Swap with the call:

```
Swap(List(i),List(Min));
```

The actual parameter List(i) corresponds to the formal parameter a, while List(min) corresponds to b.

In *named* association, the procedure call explicitly names the formal parameter and its associated actual parameter. The ordering doesn't matter. Procedure calls equivalent to the call to Swap above (but using named parameter association) are:

```
Swap( a => List(i), b => List(Min));
```

and

```
Swap( b => List(Min), a => List(i));
```

In procedure calls using both associations, the positional parameters must precede the named.

Parameter-Passage Modes

Formal parameters to procedures have one of three modes: **in**, **out**, or **in out**.

in	The formal parameter is a constant initialized to the value of the actual parameter. Because it is a constant, the parameter's value can only be accessed or used; it may not be assigned.
in out	The formal parameter is a variable that allows its value to be both accessed and assigned.
out	The formal parameter is a variable whose value can only be assigned; it may not be accessed or used.

For scalars, these parameter-passage modes are implemented by a technique called *copy-in copy-out*. When a procedure is called, the in and in out formal parameters are assigned the values of their corresponding actual parameters. When a procedure terminates, the values of in out and out formal parameters are assigned back to their actual parameters.

Superficially the in mode is like the "pass-by-value" technique of Pascal or C. The difference is that pass-by-value formal parameters are variables, whereas **in** formal parameters are constants. Similarly in out mode may seem like pass-by-reference in Pascal or Modula-2. However, in pass-by-reference, a change to the formal parameter results in a simultaneous change to the actual parameter. With in out mode, the actual parameter is not updated until the procedure terminates and the value of the formal parameter is copied out.

The copy-in copy-out rules apply only to parameters having a simple scalar type. Access types use copy-in for all three modes, and Ada compilers are allowed (but not required) to pass arrays and records using pass-by-reference.

An in formal parameter may have a default value. In this case, an actual parameter may be omitted and the default value used. Positional parameter associations may not follow such an ommission.

Example

Given the procedure:

```
procedure Incr(N: in out Integer; Amt: in Integer := 1) is
            -- Increase N by Amt.
begin
N := N + Amt;
end Incr;
```

the following calls are valid:

```
Incr(Z,4);       -- Increment Z by 4.
Incr(K);         -- Increment K by 1.
```

The Return Statement

The **return** statement is used to terminate a procedure or function and transfer control back to the calling routine. The syntax is:

return_statement ::= **return** [expression];

A procedure may contain any number of **return** statements, none of which may contain the indicated optional expression. If it has no return statement, the procedure terminates after the execution of the sequence of statements making up its body. The [expression] is used in function subprograms to indicate the value returned.

Example

```
procedure Min(a,b: in Integer; c: out Integer) is
     -- Return through c the smaller of a and b.
begin
if (a < b) then
     c := a;
      return;
end if;
c := b;
end Min;
```

6.3 FUNCTIONS

Declaration/Body

Simplified syntax for function declarations and bodies is:

subprogram_declaration ::= subprogram_specification;

subprogram_specification ::=
                    function designator [formal_part] **return** type

subprogram_body ::=
        function designator [formal_part] **return** type **is**
              [declarative_part]
        begin
              sequence_of_statements

> **end** [designator];
>
> designator ::= designator | operator_symbol

As with procedures, function declarations are used to provide the function name, parameter requirements, and return type to other compilation units, and as forward declarations. Notice that the data type of the value returned by the function is declared in its specification. The return value may be any type, including an array or record. Also, the formal parameters are restricted to the mode **in**.

The body of a function must contain at least one **return** statement. All return statements must have the form:

> **return** expression;

The value of the expression is returned as the function value and must have the correct return type.

Examples

A **function** declaration:

```
function Is_Digit(Char : in Character) return Boolean;
```

A **function** body:

```
function Is_Digit(Char : in Character) return Boolean is
begin
        return (Char in '0'..'9');
end Is_Digit;
```

Function Calls

A function is invoked by its name. Simplified syntax is:

> function_call ::=
>
>   function_name [actual_parameter_part];

> actual_parameter_part ::=
>
>   (parameter_association {, parameter_association})

Parameters are optional and may be either *positional* or *named*, but if present, are listed within parentheses and separated by commas. Unlike a procedure call, a function call is not a statement. Rather, the call appears in an expression where the value returned by the function is used. For example, the function Is_Digit in the previous section could be called within a Boolean expression, such as:

```
if (Is_Digit(Ch)) then
    ...
end if;
```

As another example of a function, here is a complete program that prints a table of square roots.

```
with Text_IO; use Text_IO;
procedure Table is
    package Flt_IO is new Float_IO(Float); use Flt_IO;

    function Sqrt(X: in Float) return Float is
         -- Use Newton's Method to calculate an
         -- approximation to the square root of x.
      X_n      : Float := X;       -- nth approximation.
      X_nplus1 : Float := X/2.0  -- (n+1)st approximation.
    begin
    if (X < 0.0) then
          Put_Line("square root error - negative argument");
          return (-1.0);
    elsif (X = 0.0) then
          return (0.0);
    end if;
    while abs(X_n - X_nplus1) > 0.00001 loop
          X_n := X_nplus1;
          X_nplus1 := 0.5 * (X_n + X / X_n);
    end loop;
    return X_nplus1;
    end Sqrt;

begin
for i in 1..100 loop
    Put( Float(i) ,4,2,0);
    Put( Sqrt(Float(i)), 4,4,0);
    New_Line;
end loop;
end Table;
```

Infix Functions

Functions can be written so that they are called using conventional infix notation for the binary operators ****, abs, not, *, /, rem, mod, +, -, &, =, <=, >=, <, >, <>, and, or,** and the unary operators **+, -.**

For example, a function called *"*"* can be written to multiply two matrixes. It would be called to multiply matrixes A and B to yield C with the statement:

```
C := A * B;
```

Example

```
type Matrix is array(1..5,1..5) of Float;

function "*"(A,B : in Matrix) return Matrix is
    C : Matrix;
```

```
begin
for i in 1..5 loop
    for j in 1..5 loop
        C(i,j) := 0.0;
        for k in 1..5 loop
            C(i,j) := C(i,j) + A(i,k) * B(k,j);
        end loop;
    end loop;
end loop;
return C;
end "*";     -- End of matrix multiply function.
```

Notice that the operator appears between quotes in the function specification. There are some restrictions on the use of infix operators. An equality function using "=" is allowed only if it has a `Boolean` return type and both parameters have the same limited type. An inequality function called "/=" may not be written explicitly, but rather is available automatically for each "=" operation and provides an opposite result.

6.4 OVERLOADING OF SUBPROGRAM NAMES

Ada permits programs to contain and use subprograms having the same identifier name. Such a name is said to be *overloaded*. An example of an overloaded name is `Put` provided in `Text_IO`. `Text_IO` contains procedures for the output of `String`, `Integer`, `Character`, and `Float` data; yet they all have the same name, `Put`. When a program calls a `Put` procedure, a compiler can tell which `Put` is being called by the number and types of the actual parameters. For example, it is obvious that the procedure call `Put("Ada")` is referring to the string version of `Put`.

The number and corresponding base types of the formal parameters to a subprogram are called its *parameter-type profile*. The *profile* of a subprogram consists of both its parameter-type profile and its return-value base type (in the case of functions). Subprogram names can be overloaded as long as the subprograms have different profiles. Notice that this allows functions to have the same name and same parameter type profile as long as their return base types are different.

6.5 RECURSION

Both procedures and functions may be called recursively; that is, they may call themselves. Below are two examples:

```
function Fact(n : in Integer) return Integer is
    -- Return n!, assumes n >= 0.
```

```
begin
if (n = 0) then
    return 1;
else
    return  n * Fact(n-1);
end Fact;

procedure Sum(A: in ArrayType;
                   i,j: in Integer; S: out Integer) is
        -- Sum the elements of A in range i..j,
        -- return result through S, assume i <= j.
    RearSum : Integer;
begin
if (i = j) then
      S := A(i);
else
      Sum(A,i+1,j,RearSum); -- Sum from i+1 to j
      S := A(i) + RearSum;
end if;
end Sum;
```

6.6 SCOPE AND VISIBILITY RULES

The term **scope** refers to the portion of a program where an object such as a subprogram, variable, or type may legally be referenced and thus used. The rules of *visibility* specify if and how one refers to an object throughout its scope. In this section, Ada's scope and visibility rules are covered, with discussion restricted to objects declared within subprograms.

The scope of an object begins immediately after its declaration and terminates at the end of the subprogram in which it is declared. Thus, for a sequence of subprograms declared within another, a subprogram may not be called before its point of declaration (hence the need for occasional forward declarations). Likewise the scope of a variable is restricted to the subprogram in which it is declared. The scope of a **for** loop parameter begins when it appears and terminates at the end of its loop.

An object can have one of three types of visibility (which can vary) throughout its scope. An object that is *directly visible* can be referenced by its identifier name. This is the default visibility of an object. The object becomes *visible by selection* when a nested subprogram or **for** loop parameter redefines the identifier of the object. The object can then be referenced if its name is prefixed by the subprogram in which it is declared (see example below). An object becomes *hidden* when it cannot be referenced at all within its scope. This occurs to a **for** loop parameter whose loop contains another **for** loop parameter with the same identifier name.

The procedure in Figure 6.1 illustrates the scope and visibility rules.

```
procedure P1 is                 — start of P1's scope

    x : Integer;                — start of x's scope
    y : Integer;                — start of y's scope


    procedure P2 is             — start of P2's scope
        x : Integer;            — start of x of P2 scope
    begin
    x := 4;                     — x of P2 is directly visible
    P1.x := 3;                  — x of P1 is visible by selection
    y := 7;                     — y of P1 is directly visible
    end P2;                     — end of x of P2 scope


    procedure P3 is             — start of P3's scope
        y : Integer;            — start of y of P3 scope
    begin
    x := 5;                     — x of P1 is directly visible
    y := 7;                     — y of P3 is directly visible
    P1.y := 2;                  — y of P1 is visible by selection
    P2;                         — P2 is directly visible
    end P3;                     — end of y of P3 scope


begin
P3;                             — P3 is directly visible
x := 6;                         — x of P1 is directly visible
for i in 1..3 loop              — start of outer i's scope
    for i in 1..5 loop          — start in inner i's scope,
                                — outer i is hidden here
        . . .
    end loop;                   — end of inner i's scope
end loop;                       — end of outer i's scope
end P1;   — end of scope for x and y of P1, and P2, and P3
```

FIGURE 6.1 Illustration of slope and visibility rules

6.7 SUBPROGRAM LIBRARIES

Ada encourages the development and use of reusable code by requiring a programming environment in which libraries of code can be easily maintained. In this section, we will discuss library units produced from subprograms. Later chapters will cover the use of packages and generics in libraries.

Separate Compilation

Subprogram declarations, subprogram bodies, and main procedures can be compiled separately and are then placed in a *program library*. For example, consider the declarations of the following subprograms, CubeInt and CubeFlt.

```
-- Subprograms to return the cube of a number.

function CubeInt(a: in Integer) return Integer;
procedure CubeFlt(a: in Float; cube_a: out Float);
```

The declarations could be stored in a file and compiled separately from the file containing the corresponding subprogram bodies. These are shown below.

```
function CubeInt(a: in Integer) return Integer is
        -- Return the cube of a.
begin
return (a*a*a);
end CubeInt;

procedure CubeFlt(a: in Float; Cube_a: out Float) is
        -- Return through Cube_a, the cube of a.
begin
Cube_a := a*a*a;
end CubeFlt;
```

Another compilation unit can indicate its intent to use CubeInt or CubeFlt through the use of a **with** clause. As an example, the following main procedure cubes two numbers.

```
with  Text_IO, CubeInt, CubeFlt;
use   Text_IO;

procedure Driver is          -- Test the cube routines.

    package Flt_IO is new Float_IO(Float);     use Flt_IO;
    package Int_IO is new Integer_IO(Integer); use Int_IO;

    Int_Num : Integer;
    Flt_Num, Flt_Cubed : Float;

begin
Put('Enter an Integer '); Get(Int_Num);
Put(Int_Num,4); Put(" cubed = "); Put(CubeInt(Int_Num),6);
New_Line;
```

```
Put("Enter a Floating point number "); Get(Flt_Num);
CubeFlt(Flt_Num,Flt_Cubed);
Put(Flt_Num,4,3,0); Put(" cubed = "); Put(Flt_Cubed,6,3,0);
New_Line;
end Driver;
```

All subprograms are not sufficiently general to warrant separate compilation. But many are, including math functions, IO routines, and sorting routines.

Advantages of Compiling Declarations

Compiling subprogram declarations is not required. But if they are compiled, a compilation unit that uses the subprograms can be compiled before the subprogram bodies are even written. This allows the development of both programs to proceed at the same time, an advantage when groups of programmers are working on a large software system.

Another advantage is that the subprogram bodies can be changed and recompiled (perhaps to produce more efficient code) and as long as the declarations don't change, it is not necessary to recompile the programs that use them. Of course, the programs do need to be linked again to produce a new executable program, but the compilation of the unchanged programs can be skipped. Again, this speeds the development of large systems.

7

ACCESS TYPES

7.1 INTRODUCTION

`Access` types permit the creation of dynamic variables. Unlike other variables, which are automatically created when a program unit is entered, dynamic variables can be created at any time they are needed by using an *allocator* operation. This operation allocates memory space for the variable and stores its address in an access-type variable. Thus the access variable can "access" the dynamically created variable.

Often called *pointer types* in other languages, `access` types are used to create linked lists, trees, graphs, and a variety of other "linked" structures. This chapter shows how to declare and use `access` type variables.

7.2 DECLARATIONS AND ALLOCATORS

The syntax for declaring access types is:

    access_type_definition ::= **access** subtype_indication

The subtype_indication specifies the type of the dynamic variable an access variable can access (or point to).

Example type declarations

```
type CharPtr is access Character;

type Vector is array(1..4) of Integer;
type VecPtr is access Vector;

type Stat is record
                Age : Integer;
                Weight : Float;
                Height : Float;
            end record;
type StatPtr is access Stat;
```

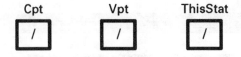

FIGURE 7.1 Illustration of access variables with value null

Having declared the access types, variables of these types can be declared.

Examples

```
Cpt       : CharPtr;
Vpt       : VecPtr;
ThisStat : StatPtr;
```

Access variables are, by default, initialized to the access value null. Null is an Ada access-type literal, indicating that the variable does not currently access (point to) any dynamic variable. An access variable having value null is often visualized with a slash (/) in a cell, as shown in Figure 7.1. Dynamic variables are created by the Ada allocator operation new. Simplified syntax for the new allocator is:

allocator ::=
          new subtype_indication | **new** qualified_expression

The allocator new can be thought of as a function that allocates memory space for a variable and returns its address to an access variable. This address is not available for use by a programmer. Also, access types can be used only with variables dynamically created with new. The dynamic variable is referenced by the name of the access variable followed by ".all".

Examples of allocations using a *subtype_indication*

```
Cpt := new Integer;
Vpt := new Vector;
ThisStat := new Stat;
```

Figure 7.2 shows the allocations. Cpt.all has type Character, Vpt.all has type Vector, and ThisStat.all has type Stat. These variables may be assigned values by referencing them using standard Ada naming conventions.

Examples

```
Cpt.all := 'x';
for i in 1..4 loop
    Vpt.all(i) := 2*i;
end loop;
ThisStat.all.Age := 25;
ThisStat.all.Weight := 120.5;
ThisStat.all.Height := 5.75;
```

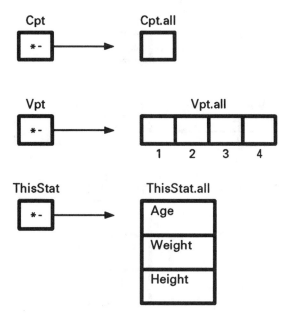

FIGURE 7.2

For arrays and records, selected components may be referenced without the
".all" notation.

Examples (equivalent to those above)

```
for i in 1..4 loop
    Vpt(i) := 2*i;
end loop;
ThisStat.Age := 25;
ThisStat.Weight := 120.5;
ThisStat.Height := 5.75;
```

Dynamic variables can be initialized at the time of their allocation using a *qualified_expression*. A qualified expression has the syntax:

qualified_expression ::=

           type_mark'(expression) | type_mark'aggregate

Examples of allocation with qualified_expression

```
Cpt := new Character'('x');
Vpt := new Vector'(2,4,6,8);
ThisStat := new Stat'(25,120.5,5.75);
```

Figure 7.3 shows these allocations. Access variables can be compared using "="
and "/=" to determine if they access the same object. In addition, assignments

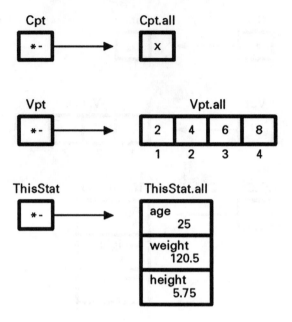

FIGURE 7.3

can be made between them so that they do access the same object. It is also possible to make allocations when access variables are declared. The declarations below declare access variables Vpt1 and Vpt2, and allocate and initialize arrays for them to access.

```
Vpt1 : VecPtr := new Vector'(2,4,6,8);
Vpt2 : VecPtr := new Vector'(1,3,5,7);
```

Figure 7.4 shows these declarations. Having allocated the arrays, the assignments below show the difference between assignments involving access variables and assignments involving the variables they access.

The assignment: Vpt1 := Vpt2 results in Figure 7.5.

The assignment: Vpt1.**all** := Vpt2.**all** results in Figure 7.6.

7.3 LINKED DATA STRUCTURES

Access types provide a flexible method for implementing linked structures of all kinds. A linked data structure is a collection of nodes in which each node contains "pointers" to other nodes. In Ada, these pointers are access variables.

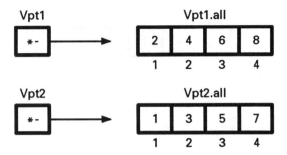

FIGURE 7.4

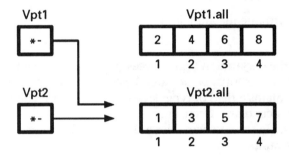

FIGURE 7.5 The result of the assignment Vpt1:= Vpt2

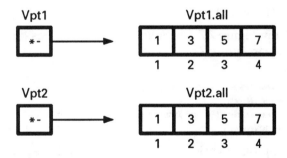

FIGURE 7.6 The result of the assignment Vpt1.**all** := Vpt2.**all**

Linked Lists

A linked list is a linear structure in which each node contains a pointer to the next node in the list. Type declarations for a node containing an integer, a character, and a pointer to the next node are:

Head

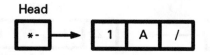

FIGURE 7.7

```
type Node;
type NodePtr  is access Node;
type Node is record
                IntVal : Integer;
                Char    : Character;
                Next    : NodePtr;
            end record;
```

The declarations start with the incomplete type declaration:

```
type Node;
```

This is needed so that the declaration for the access type NodePtr can reference the type name Node. NodePtr must be declared before the full type declaration of Node because this contains a field of type NodePtr. The incomplete type declaration of Node solves a circular-referencing problem.

To create the linked list, access variables are needed. These are declared in the usual manner, for example:

```
Head, ThisNode : NodePtr;
```

The code:

```
Head := new Node'(1,'A',null);
```

creates the one-node list in Figure 7.7. The following code finishes the creation of a three-node list shown in Figure 7.8.

```
ThisNode := Head;
ThisNode.Next := new Node'(2,'d',null);
ThisNode := ThisNode.Next;
ThisNode.Next := new Node'(3,'a',null);
ThisNode := ThisNode.Next;
```

As another example, the program below reads a line of text, stores it in a singly linked list and prints it out. The first node of the list is a "dummy" sentinel node to simplify the code.

```
with Text_IO;  use  Text_IO;
procedure LinkTest is

    type Link;
    type LinkPtr is access Link;
    type Link is record
                Char : Character;
                Next : LinkPtr;
            end record;
```

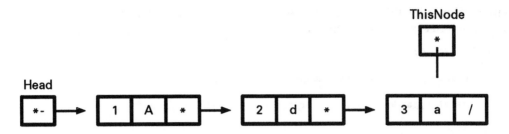

FIGURE 7.8

```
        Head : LinkPtr := new Link'(' ',null);
        Tail : LinkPtr := Head;  -- Tail starts out pointing to
                                 -- the sentinel node.
     Ch : Character;
begin
while (not End_Of_Line) loop    -- Tail is used to create
     Get(Ch);                   -- a new last node, and
     Tail.Next := new Link'(Ch,null);  -- then set to
     Tail := Tail.Next;               -- point to it.
end loop;
Tail := Head;   -- Now set Tail back to the sentinel
while (Tail.Next /= null) loop   -- and have it travel the
     Tail := Tail.Next;          -- list, printing each
     Put(Tail.Ch);              -- character.
end loop;
New_Line;
end LinkTest.
```

By adding access variables to list nodes, it is possible to create a variety of structures such as doubly linked lists, trees, and graphs.

Binary Trees

A binary tree is a linked structure that is either empty or contains a node (called the root node), along with two disjoint trees, called the left and right subtrees of the root. A structure to implement a binary tree of integers is:

```
type TreeNode;
type NodePtr is access TreeNode;
type TreeNode is record
                Num    : Integer;
                Lchild : NodePtr;
                Rchild : NodePtr;
            end record;
```

Each node of the tree contains pointers to its left and right subtrees. The roots of these subtrees are respectively called the left and right children of the node. The

program below uses this structure to read in a list of integers, store them in a
binary search tree, and print them out in ascending order.

```
with Text_IO;  use Text_IO;
program BinTree is
    package Int_IO is new Integer_IO(Integer); use Int_IO;

    -- !! type declarations for the tree structure go here !!

    Root  : NodePtr;   -- Points to the root of the tree.
    Value : Integer;   -- Used to read integers from input.

    procedure Attach(Root: in out NodePtr; Val: in Integer) is
        -- Recursive procedure to attach a node to a binary
        -- search tree. The node is added as a leaf node.
    begin
    if (Root = null) then     -- Add node to an empty tree.
       Root := new TreeNode'(Val,null,null);
    elsif (Val < Root.Num) then   -- Add node to left subtree.
       Attach(Root.Lchild,Val);
    else                          -- Add node to right subtree.
       Attach(Root.Rchild,Val);
    end if;
    end Attach;

    procedure InOrder(Root: in NodePtr) is
        -- A recursive inorder traversal of the tree
    begin
    if (Root /= null) then
       InOrder(Root.Lchild);
       Put(Root.Num,4); New_Line;
       InOrder(Root.Rchild);
    end if;
    end InOrder;

begin
loop
    Put("Enter an integer (0 to quit): ");
    Get(Value);
    exit when (Value = 0);
    Attach(Root,Value);         -- Add the integer to the tree
end loop;
New_Line;
InOrder(Root);  -- Traverse the tree in order.
end BinTree;
```

7.4 UNCHECKED DEALLOCATION

A dynamic variable created with the **new** allocator will remain allocated as long
as it can be directly or indirectly accessed through an access variable. An Ada

implementation has the option of providing a garbage-collection scheme to retrieve memory space that was allocated but is no longer accessible. This can produce unacceptable consequences in some programming situations. For example, since garbage collection is optional, it cannot be depended upon to prevent a program from exhausting all its available memory space. A problem could then arise with a program's portability. Even if garbage collection is provided, when and how often it is performed, and how long it takes, is controlled by the Ada run-time system. Unpredictable pauses of unpredictable lengths could occur during a program's execution as garbage collection is performed. This could adversely affect interactive or real-time programs.

To allow programmer control over the deallocation of dynamic variables, Ada provides two features. The first is a **pragma** (compiler directive) called Controlled that explicity disables garbage collection for a specified access type. The second is a generic procedure called unchecked_deallocation that allows the programmer to return the memory space used by a dynamic variable.

The **pragma** Controlled has the form:

```
pragma Controlled(access_type);
```

Notice that the name of the access type being controlled is an argument to the **pragma**. A program declaring several access types requires such a **pragma** for each type being controlled.

The procedure unchecked_deallocation is a generic library routine. To use it, a program must contain the **with** clause:

```
with unchecked_deallocation;
```

and must instantiate a deallocation procedure for each access type being controlled. The syntax for such an instantiation is:

procedure identifier
 is new unchecked_deallocation(object_type,access_type);

Notice that both the access type and the type of the object being accessed are arguments to the instantiation. The following declarations and code segment illustrate how to use these Ada features.

Example

```
type Link;
type LinkPtr is access Link;
type Link is record
              Char : Character;
              Next : LinkPtr;
          end record;
         ...
Head : LinkPtr
pragma Controlled(LinkPtr);
procedure Free is new unchecked_deallocation(Link,LinkPtr);
```

```
        ...
Head := new Link'('A',null);   -- Allocate a variable.
        ...
Free(Head);-- Deallocate a variable.
```

Notice that the argument to the procedure Free is the access variable for the dynamic variable being deallocated. Also, upon return from the procedure Free, the access variable Head has value null.

If two or more access variables access the same object, only one of them is used in a deallocation procedure to reclaim memory space. This access variable becomes null and the others are then undefined. For this reason, the procedure to reclaim memory is called *unchecked*. It would be an error for a program to attempt to use the values of these undefined access variables.

8 PACKAGES

8.1 INTRODUCTION

A **package** is a program unit that allows a collection of related entities to be made available for use by other program units. These entities could be constants, variables, types, procedures, functions, exceptions, or tasks. Packages support programming concepts such as modular and reusable code, abstract data types, and information hiding. An illustrative example is the supplied package `Text_IO`. `Text_IO` provides the data types, procedures and functions for performing input and output with text files. The implementation details of how all this is accomplished are hidden, in fact, they are of no concern to a programmer.

There are generally two parts to a package: a *specification* and a *body*. A *package specification* contains declarations indicating the entities being made available by the package. It is the public or visible part of the package (although it may contain some information that is private and hence hidden from other program units.) A *package body* contains the implementation details for these entities and is hidden from a program unit that uses the package. So, for example, while a procedure declaration would appear in a specification, its body, which includes the statement sequence it executes, would be in the package body.

8.2 PACKAGE SPECIFICATIONS AND BODIES

The syntax for a package specification is:

```
package_declaration  ::= package_specification;
package_specification  ::= package identifier is
                                    { basic_declarative_item }
                           [ private
                                    { basic_declarative_item } ]
                               end identifier
```

As an example, a specification for a package called MathNums that provides a collection of mathematical constants is:

```
package MathNums is
     Pi  : constant := 3.14159265;
     Exp : constant := 2.718281828;
     Degrees_Per_Radian : constant := 57.295779;
end MathNums;
```

This specification can be compiled and then used by any program. A program indicates that it is using the package by the **with** clause:

```
with MathNums;
```

Example program using the MathNums package

```
with Text_IO; use Text_IO;
with MathNums;

procedure Circle is
     -- A program to compute the area of a circle.

        package Flt_IO; is new Float_IO(Float); use Flt_IO;

Radius, Area : Float;

begin
Put('Enter the radius of a circle: ');
Get(Radius);
Area := MathNums.Pi * Radius * Radius;   -- Compute area.
Put('The area of the circle is: ');
Put(Area,5,3,0);
end Circle;
```

Notice that the constant Pi is referenced by the name of the package it is from, followed by a period ("."), followed by its name.

```
MathNums.Pi
```

This notation clearly exhibits the package containing the constant and provides useful documentation in a program that uses several packages, some of which might duplicate names of objects. A **use** clause allows a package object to be referenced without the package name. So, if the program above contained:

```
with MathNums;   use MathNums;
```

the formula for computing the area of the circle could have been:

```
Area := Pi * Radius * Radius;
```

As another example, a specification for a package providing random-number generators is:

```
package RandPkg is
    function Random_Flt return Float;
        -- Return random Float in range [0,1).
    function Random_Int(Lo,Hi: in Integer) return Integer;
        -- Return random Integer in range [Lo,Hi].
end RandPkg;
```

A program using this package is provided with functions returning pseudo-random `Float` and `Integer` numbers. This package must have a package body containing the implementation details. The body must be compiled so that it is added to the *program library*.

Simplified syntax for a package body is:

```
package body identifier is
    [declarative part]
[begin
    sequence_of_statements]
end identifier;
```

The *declarative part* of the body can contain type and variable declarations in addition to the bodies of the subprograms appearing in the package specification. There may also be additional subprograms, not accessible to a user of the package, but necessary to implement the package. The optional *sequence_of_statements* is executed prior to the execution of any main program and can be used to initialize the package.

The body of `RandPkg` is:

```
with Calendar; use Calendar;

package body RandPkg is

    Seed : Float; -- Seed of the random-number generator;

    procedure Randomize is
        -- Initializes the seed.
    begin
    Seed := Float(Seconds(Clock)) * 0.341659;
    Seed := Float(Seed - Float(Integer(Seed - 0.5)));
    end Randomize;

    function Random_Flt return Float is
        x : Float;
    begin
    x := (Seed + 3.141659);
    x := x * x * x * x * x;
    Seed := Float(x - Float(Integer(x - 0.5)));
    return (Seed);
    end Random_Flt;
```

```
function Random_Int(Lo, Hi: in Integer) return Integer is
    x : Float;
begin
x := Random_Flt;
return Integer((Float(Hi-Lo+1)*x+Float(Lo)-0.5));
end Random_Int;

begin
Randomize;    -- Call to initialize the seed.
end RandPkg;
```

Notice that the package body uses the function Clock, from the required compilation unit Calendar, to initialize the seed of the random-number generator. Also, the variable Seed and procedure Randomize are local to the package body and thus hidden from and inaccessible to a program unit using the package.

Below is a complete driver program to test RandPkg.

```
with Text_IO; use Text_IO;
with RandPkg;
    Test the random-number package.
procedure RandTest is

    use RandPkg;
    package Flt_IO is new Float_IO(Float); use Flt_IO;
    package Int_IO is new Integer_IO(Integer); use Int_IO;

begin--  Print several random numbers.
for i in 1..10 loop
    Put(Random_Flt,2,6,0); New_Line; -- Generate Floats.
end loop;
Put_Line("----------");
for i in 1..10 loop
    Put(Random_Int(1,100),6); New_Line;   -- Generate integers.
end loop;
end RandTest;
```

8.3 PRIVATE AND LIMITED PRIVATE TYPES

An Example

It is possible to hide the implementation details of a data type appearing in the visible part of a package specification by declaring it a **private** type. The actual implementation would then appear in the **private** section. The syntax of the declaration is:

private_type_declaration ::=
        type identifier [discriminant_part] **is** [limited] **private**;

Consider the following specification for a package implementing a stack of integers. The declaration:

```
type Stack is private;
```

hides the full type declaration from a program unit using the package.

```
package StackPkg is
    type Stack is private;
    function Empty(s: in Stack) return Boolean;
    function Full(s: in Stack) return Boolean;
    procedure Push(s: in out Stack; Num: in Integer);
    procedure Pop(s: in out Stack; Num: out Integer);
    procedure Top(s: in Stack; Num: in Integer);
private
    type Node;
    type Stack is access node;        -- A stack will be a
    type Node is record               -- linked list of nodes
                Data : Integer;       -- with a pointer to
                Next : Stack;         -- the top of the stack.
             end record;
end StackPkg;
```

A program unit using this package could declare variables of type `Stack` and operate on them using the stack routines `Push`, `Pop`, `Empty`, etc. The program could not, however, make use of the fact that the stack is implemented as a pointer to a linked list. This allows a programmer to hide implementation details of an object (such as a stack) from a user of the package. In particular, the type `Node` is not visible outside of the package.

A portion of the body of the package would be:

```
package body StackPkg is

    function Empty(s: in Stack) return Boolean is
    begin
        return (s = null);
    end Empty;

    procedure Push(s: in out Stack; Num: in Stack) is
    begin
        s := new Node'(Num,s); -- Link to front of list.
    end Push;
        ...
end StackPkg;
```

Operations on Private Types

Outside of the package in which they are declared, the operations on objects having a private type are restricted to assignments, tests for equality and inequality, and operations involving discriminants, such as using a discriminant, to select record components.

Limited Private Types and ADTs

A type in the visible part of a package specification can be declared **limited private**. The declaration form is:

> **type** identifier **is limited private**;

Operations on objects of these types are restricted to those provided by the procedures and functions of the package itself. In particular, assignment and the relational operators (such as equality, less than, etc.) are not allowed. These operations must be supplied by subprograms in the package. Of course, Boolean functions can overload operators like equality, "=".

An abstract data type (ADT) is an entity having a collection of possible data values, along with a set of operations on these values. Common examples include stacks, queues, trees, and symbol tables. Limited private types provide support for ADTs.

The Stack package described in this section should have declared the type Stack as `limited private`. The declaration in the specification would then be:

> **type** Stack **is limited private**;

The reason for this is to prevent a user of the package from using it in a manner that could lead to logical errors. For example, when declared as a `private` type, assignments could be made between stacks using the assignment operator ":=". But what does this mean? Does it produce a copy of the stack as ":=" does with other data types? With the linked-list stack implementation it clearly does not, but with an array implementation it would. By declaring stack as `limited private`, the user of the package is completely insulated from these issues. The user could write his/her own stack assignment procedure, or it could have been supplied with the package as an additional stack operation.

9

GENERIC UNITS

9.1 INTRODUCTION

It is not uncommon to need several essentially similar subprograms or packages. For example, different sorting procedures are required to sort arrays of integers, arrays of floating-point numbers, arrays of characters, and arrays of records. The algorithm used for the sort could be the same for each procedure; the only differences would be the type of data involved, the array index range, and how the ordering of the elements is defined. Rather than requiring the coding of virtually identical procedures, Ada permits the creation of a template containing the sort algorithm. This template is called a `generic` procedure. Through a process called *instantiation*, specific instances of the procedure can be obtained for a given type and size array and ordering of elements. The array type, index range, and element ordering function are actual parameters corresponding to generic formal parameters.

Ada supports `generic` procedures, functions, and packages. Their use saves programming time and effort and encourages the design of general-purpose, reusable program modules. This chapter covers the declaration and use of generic units.

9.2 AN EXAMPLE OF A GENERIC UNIT

There are three aspects to defining and then using a generic unit: the generic unit declaration, the generic subprogram or package body, and the instantiation of an instance of the generic unit.

The declaration includes a specification of both the generic formal parameters and the generic subprogram or package. Below is the declaration and body of a generic `swap` procedure that interchanges the value of two variables.

A Generic Declaration

```
generic
    type Item is private;   -- Item is a formal type parameter.
procedure GenericSwap(x,y: in out Item);
                         --Generic subprogram declaration.
```

A Generic Body

```
procedure GenericSwap(x,y: in out Item) is
                    -- Interchange x and y.
    Temp : Item := x;
begin
    x := y;
    y := Temp;
end GenericSwap;
```

To use a generic unit, a program uses a `with` clause and instantiates an instance of `swap` for each desired type.

Generic Instantiations

```
with GenericSwap;
    ...
    type ArrayType is array ...
    type RecordType is record ...
    ...
procedure Swap is new GenericSwap(Integer);
procedure Swap is new GenericSwap(Float);
procedure Swap is new GenericSwap(Character);
procedure Swap is new GenericSwap(ArrayType);
procedure Swap is new GenericSwap(RecordType);
```

The code above creates five instances of the `GenericSwap` procedure, all called `Swap`. The actual parameters to the instantiations are `Integer`, `Float`, `Character`, `ArrayType`, and `RecordType`. They each in turn correspond to the generic formal parameter `Item`. Notice that the name `Swap` is overloaded. Once the swap procedures have been instantiated, they may be called in the usual manner using their name, `Swap`.

The declaration and body can be compiled separately or together. The declaration must appear or be compiled before the body.

9.3 GENERIC DECLARATIONS

Declaration Form

A generic declaration consists of two sections: a list of the formal parameters to the generic unit and the subprogram or package specification. The syntax is:

    generic_declaration ::= generic_specification;

where

generic_specification ::=
>   generic_formal_part subprogram_specification |
>   generic_formal_part package_specification

generic_formal_part ::=
>   **generic** {generic_parameter_declaration}

generic_parameter_declaration ::=
>   identifier_list : [**in** [**out**]] type [:= expression]; |
>   **type** identifier **is** generic_type_definition |
>   private_type_declaration |
>   **with** subprogram_specification [**is** name]; |
>   **with** subprogram_specification [**is** <>];

generic_type_definition ::=
>   (<>) | **range** <> | **digits** <> | **delta** <> |
>   array_type_definition | access_type_definition

Examples

```
            -- Declaration of a generic swap procedure.
generic
     type Item is private;      -- Data type parameter.
procedure GenericSwap(a,b : in out Item);
```

```
            -- Declaration of a generic sort procedure.
generic
     type Item is private;    -- Array element-type parameter.
     type Index is (<>);      -- Array index-type parameter.
     type Vector is array(Index range <>) of Item;
                              -- Unconstrained-array parameter.
     with function "<"(x,y: in Item) return Boolean;
                              -- Element-ordering parameter.
procedure SortList(List : in out Vector);
```

```
     -- Declaration of generic integer array summing function.
generic
     type Element is range <>; -- Array-element parameter.
     type Vector is array(Integer range <>) of Element;
                              -- Array parameter.
function Sum(List : in out Vector) return Integer;
```

```
                    -- Declaration of generic stack package.
generic
     type Item is private;        -- Stack item-type parameter.
     Size : in Integer := 50;     -- Max stack-size parameter
                                  -- with default size of 50.
package StackPkg is
     type Stack is limited private;
     function Empty(s: in out Stack) return Boolean;
     procedure Push(s: in out Stack; e: in Item);
     procedure Pop(s: in out Stack; e: out Item);
private
     type Vector is array(1..Size) of Item;
     type Stack is
              record
                  List : Vector; -- Storage for stack items.
                  Top : Integer := 0; -- Index of top item.
              end record;
end StackPkg;
```

Generic Value and Type Parameters

Ordinary formal parameters using passage modes in and in out are allowed in generic units. Only the in mode is discussed here. Such a parameter acts as a constant in the generic unit. An example is the parameter Size in the generic stack package of the last section. Size is used to set the capacity of the stack.

Seven kinds of formal data type parameters are allowed (examples from the last section are noted):

(1) A [limited] private type. (See Item in StackPkg.)

(2) An array type. (See Vector in Sum and SortList.)

(3) An access type. (Allocators may be used.)

(4) Discrete types (denoted by "(<>)".) (See Index in SortList).

(5) Integer types (denoted by "range <>") (See Element in Sum.)

(6) Floating-point types (denoted by "digits <>").

(7) Fixed-point types (denoted by "delta <>");

Examples

```
type Item is private;
type Index is (<>);
type List is array(DiscreteRange) of Item;
type Height is digits <>;        -- A floating-point type.
type Amount is delta <>;         -- A fixed-point type.
type AgeRange is range <>;       -- An integer type.
```

The kind of formal type parameter determines the operations permitted on objects of that type within the body of a generic unit. Consider, for example, the formal type parameter

```
type Index is (<>);
```

which specifies that `Index` is a discrete type. Only operations common to all discrete types are allowed on objects of type `Index`. Thus the use of the relational operators and attributes such as `Val`, `Pos`, `Succ`, and `Pred` are permitted as well as the use of `Index` variables as for-loop parameters. However, the use of arithmetic operators such as '+' and '-' is invalid, even if `Index` is a numeric discrete type such as `Integer`.

Generic Subprogram Parameters

The syntax for declaring formal subprogram parameters to a generic unit is:

> with subprogram_specification [is name];

or

> with subprogram_specification [is <>];

In each case, the **is** option denotes a default subprogram.

Examples

```
with procedure Initialize(x: in out Node);
with function "<"(x,y: in Item) return Boolean;
with function "*"(x,y: in element) return Element is <>;
with procedure Update is Default_Update;
```

If **is** is followed by a subprogram name, this subprogram is the default. If **is** is followed by a box, <>, the default is the subprogram in the context of the instantiation with the same designator as the formal subprogram. For example, given the formal parameter "*" above, when the actual parameter for `Element` is `Integer`, "*" is integer multiplication. However, when the actual parameter for `Element` is `Float`, "*" is floating-point multiplication.

9.4 GENERIC BODIES

The bodies of generic subprograms and packages are the templates for the bodies of the program units instantiated from them. They are syntactically identical to a nongeneric body.

As an example, the body of the generic `Sort` procedure declared in section 9.3 is:

```
procedure SortList(List: in out Vector) is
                   -- Implements selection sort.
      Temp : Item;   -- Used to help with swapping elements.
      Min  : Index; -- Subscript of 'smallest' element.
begin
for i in List'First..Index'Pred(List'Last) loop
      Min := i;
      for j in Index'Succ(i)..List'Last loop
          if (List(j) < List(Min)) then
              Min := j;
          end if;
      end loop;

      Temp := List(i);
      List(i) := List(Min);
      List(Min) := Temp;
   end loop;
end SortList;
```

Compare this with the Sort procedure of section 6.2, in which the same algorithm is implemented. Note the extensive use of attributes in the generic sort when specifying the ranges of the for-loops. This allows the array subscripts to be from any discrete type.

9.5 GENERIC INSTANTIATION

The syntax for instantiating a generic unit is:

generic_instantiation ::=
    procedure identifier **is**
        new generic_procedure_name [generic_actual_part]; |
    function identifier **is**
        new generic_function_name [generic_actual_part]; |
    package identifier **is**
        new generic_package_name [generic_actual_part];

where the *generic_actual_part* is a list of actual parameters matching the generic formal parameters. As with actual parameters to subprograms, these may be *named* or *positional* and may be omitted for formal parameters with defaults. After such an omission, only named parameters are allowed.

A program unit using a generic unit must contain an appropriate **with** clause of the form:

with generic_procedure_name;
with generic_function_name;
with generic_package_name;

Examples of instantiations

(using the subprogram declarations of section 9.2)

```
    -- Swap procedures.
procedure Swap is new GenericSwap(Integer);
procedure Swap is new GenericSwap(Item => Float);


    -- Sort procedures and Sum function.

type IntList  is array(Integer range <>) of Integer;
subtype Digit is Character range '0'..'9'
type CharList is array(Character range <>) of Digit;
type TableEntry is record .....
type Table is array(Integer range <>) of TableEntry;
function LessThen(a,b: TableEntry) return Boolean;
                -- Ordering function for TableEntry data.

procedure Sort_Up is
          new SortList(Integer,Integer,IntList,'<');
                  -- Sort in increasing order.
procedure Sort_Down is
          new SortList(Integer,Integer,IntList,'>');
                  -- Sort in decreasing order.
procedure Sort is new SortList(Digit,Character,CharList,'<');
procedure Sort is
          new SortList(TableEntry,Integer,Table,LessThan);
function Addem is new Sum(Integer,IntList);
```

Given array variables:

```
Grades : IntList(1..50);
SymbolTable: Table(0..100);
```

The sort procedures could be called as follows:

```
Sort_Up(Grades);        -- Sort in increasing order.
Sort_Down(Grades);      -- Sort in decreasing order.
Sort_Up(Grades(1..20)); -- Sort an array slice.
Sort(SymbolTable);      -- Sort SymbolTable according to
                        -- the ordering defined by the
                        -- function LessThan.
```

Additional examples

(using the generic stack package of section 9.2.)

```
package IntStack is new StackPkg(Integer,Size => 200);
                    -- Integer stack with capacity of 200.

package CharStack is new StackPkg(Character);
                    -- Character stack with capacity of 50.
```

9.6 FORMAL PARAMETER MATCHING RULES

A generic formal **in** parameter is matched by an expression of the same type.

A generic formal **limited private** type is matched by any type.

A generic formal **private** type is matched by any type for which assignment, ":=", and equality, "=", are defined.

(<>) matches any discrete type.

range <> matches any integer type.

digits <> matches any floating-point type.

delta <> matches any fixed-point type.

A generic formal array type is matched by an actual array type having the same index type and range, and component type. Formal and actual arrays must be both constrained or unconstrained.

A generic formal access type is matched by an access type having the same object type. The object type may be a generic type.

A generic formal subprogram is matched by an actual subprogram having the same parameter and return-type profile.

9.7 ADDITIONAL EXAMPLES

A Generic Squaring Function

A generic declaration and body for a squaring function is:

```
generic
    type Item is private;
    with function '*'(u,v : Item) return Item is <>;
function Squaring(x: in Item) return Item;

function Squaring(x: in Item) return Item is
begin
    return x * x;
end Squaring;
```

Given the Matrix type and Matrix product function:

```
type Matrix is array(1..3,1..3) of Float;
function MatrixMult(A,B: Matrix) return Matrix;
```

the following instantiations are allowed:

```
function Square is new Squaring(Matrix,MatrixMult);

function Square is new Squaring(Integer);
                    -- Integer '*' is used by default.
```

```
function Square is new Squaring(Float);
                    -- Float '*' is used by default.
```

Generic Stack Package

This is a complete (albeit not robust) stack package for the example package referred to in the previous sections.

```
generic
type Item is private;       -- Stack item-type parameter.
Size : in Integer := 50;    -- Max stack-size parameter
                            -- with default size of 50.

package StackPkg is
      type Stack is limited private;
      function Empty(s: in out Stack) return Boolean;
      procedure Push(s: in out Stack; e: in Item);
      procedure Pop(s: in out Stack; e: out Item);
private
      type Vector is array(1..Size) of Item;
      type Stack is
                record
                    List : Vector; -- Storage for stack items.
                    Top : Integer := 0; -- Index of top item.
                end record;
end StackPkg;


package body StackPkg is

      function Empty(s: in out Stack) return Boolean is
      begin
          return (s.Top = 0);
      end Empty;

      procedure Push(s: in out Stack; e: in Item) is
      begin
          s.Top := s.Top + 1;
          s.List(s.Top) := e;
      end Push;

      procedure Pop(s: in out Stack; e: out Item) is
      begin
          e := s.List(s.Top);
          s.Top := s.Top - 1;
      end Pop;
end StackPkg;
```

10 ═══════════

FILES

10.1 INTRODUCTION

File services in Ada are provided by three packages. These are supplied with each Ada implementation.

Text_IO
: A package providing support for text files. Text files are sequences of characters that can be organized into lines and pages.

Sequential_IO
: A generic package providing support for sequential files. Sequential files are read-only or write-only files and contain components having the same data type.

Direct_IO
: A generic package providing support for direct-access files. Direct-access files may be read-only, read-write, or write-only and contain components having the same data type.

This chapter describes how to access and use the services in these IO packages.

10.2 ACCESSING THE IO PACKAGES

A program unit using the facilities of an IO package requires an appropriate **with** clause. These are:

```
with Text_IO;
with Sequential_IO;
with Direct_IO;
```

Of course, a program needs only a **with** clause for the package(s) it uses. Because Sequential_IO and Direct_IO are generic packages, a program must also instantiate specific packages for each file-component type required. For example, a program working with a sequential file of Integers and a direct-access file of records having type Rec_Type would have declarations such as:

```
package Seq_Int_IO is new Sequential_IO(Integer);
package Dir_Rec_IO is new Direct_IO(Rec_Type);
```

Use clauses such as:

```
use Text_IO;
use Seq_Int_IO;
use Dir_Rec_IO;
```

permit the package objects to be referenced without the package name prefix, if no ambiguity would result. In the case of subprograms, this is not a problem because procedure and function names can be overloaded.

10.3 FILE TYPES AND MODES

Each of the three IO packages supplies a data type called File_Type, which implements files. Example file declarations are:

```
TermPaper  : Text_IO.File_Type;
NumberFile : Seq_Int_IO.File_Type;
RecFile    : Dir_Rec_IO.File_Type
```

The package prefix names are required so that the compiler can distinguish to which kind of file the name File_Type refers. In a program using only one IO package and containing a corresponding use clause, the prefix can be omitted. For example:

```
TermPaper : File_Type;
```

Each package also supplies an enumeration type called File_Mode used to indicate whether a file is used for input, output, or both. The File_Mode values are:

In_File	indicates a file is read only
Inout_File	indicates a file can be both read and written
Out_File	indicates a file is write only

Only direct-access files can have the mode Inout_File.

10.4 FILE MANAGEMENT

The three standard IO packages provide procedures for creating, deleting, opening, closing, and resetting files. Each package contains the declarations of these subprograms.

The procedure Create is used to create a file. Its declaration is:

```
procedure Create(File : in out File_Type;
                 Mode : in File_Mode := default_mode;
                 Name : in String := '';
                 Form : in String := '');
```

When a file is created, it is open and initially empty. The default mode when creating text and sequential files is `Out_File`, while for direct-access files the default is `Inout_File`. The `Name`-parameter is the name of an external file associated with the file being created. If omitted, a temporary file is created that then ceases to exist when the program terminates. The `Form` parameter is system dependent and may be used to specify file characteristics such as access restrictions.

Examples (using the previous declarations)

```
Create(Termpaper);-- Create a temporary text file, opened
                  -- for output.
Create(NumberFile,Out_File,'grades.dat');-- Create a
                                         -- file of integers, associated with
                                         -- the external file grades.dat.
Create(RecFile,Inout_File,'recdata.bin');-- Create a
                                         -- file of Rec_Type, associated with
                                         -- the external file recdata.bin.
```

The procedure `Open` opens an existing file for processing, starting at the beginning of the file. Its declaration is:

```
procedure Open(File : in out File_Type;
               Mode : in File_Mode;
               Name : in String;
               Form : in String := '');
```

There is no default mode or filename when opening files. If the external file does not exist, a `Name_Error` exception is raised. Methods for handling such exceptions (so that the program does not just abort) are discussed in Chapter 12.

Examples

```
FileName : String(1..20);
     ...
Open(TermPaper,In_File,'LoveLace.Ada');
Open(RecFile,Inout_File,FileName);  -- The external file
                                    -- name is in the
                                    -- string FileName.
```

Declarations for procedures that close, delete, and reset files are:

```
procedure Close(File : in out File_Type);
procedure Delete(File : in out File_Type);
procedure Reset(File : in out File_Type);
procedure Reset(File : in out File_Type; Mode : in File_Mode);
```

Close removes the association of the Ada file with its associated external file. Delete deletes the external file associated with the given Ada file. Reset prepares the file for processing, starting with its first component. If a Mode parameter is given, the file is reset to that mode, otherwise the existing mode is used. The exception Status_Error is raised if these procedures are called and the file is not open.

There are functions for returning the mode and name of an Ada file and for determining if a file is open. See the appendixes for details.

10.5 TEXT FILES

Text files are supported by the Text_IO package. The structure of text files and their associated subprograms is covered in detail in Chapter 1, where the emphasis is placed upon the standard input and output files. The procedures and functions discussed there, such as Put, Get, End_Of_Line, and New_Line, did not specify the file being used. In this case, the default standard input and output files are assumed. Other forms of these subprograms have a file variable as the first parameter for use with other text files. Thus, given the declarations:

```
F_In  : Text_IO.File_Type;
F_Out : Text_IO.File_TYpe;
```

the function call:

```
End_Of_Line(F_In)
```

checks if the current component of the file F_In is the end-of-line indicator, while the procedure call:

```
Put_Line(F_Out,'Chapter 1');
```

writes the string "Chapter 1" to the file F_Out.

As a further example, the following code segment copies the text file paper.txt to the file paper.bak.

```
Open(F_In,In_File,'paper.txt');
Create(F_Out,Out_File,'paper.bak');
while (not End_Of_File(F_In)) loop
    while (not End_Of_Line(F_In)) loop
        Get(F_In,Char);
        Put(F_Out,Char);
    end loop;
    Skip_Line(F_In);
    New_Line(F_Out);
end loop;
Close(F_In);
Close(F_Out);
```

The generic Integer_IO and Float_IO packages also have subprogram forms accepting an initial file parameter. So, for example, having instantiated an IO package for integers, the call:

```
Put(F_Out,Count,6);
```

writes the value of the integer variable Count to the text file F_Out using a field width of 6.

Of particular interest are forms of Put and Get that read and write to strings instead of files. Given the declarations:

```
Num, Last : Integer;
Str : String(1..10);
```

the call:

```
Put(Str(1..6),Num);
```

writes the value of the variable Num to the given string, just as it would be written to a file, using the length of the string (in this case, 6) as the field width.
The call:

```
Get(Str,Num,Last);
```

reads an integer value from the beginning of the string, just as it would be read from a file, storing the value in the variable Num. Last returns with the index of the last character read. Thus given:

```
Str : String(1..10) := "34   -23  ";
```

the sequence of statements:

```
Get(Str,Num1,Last);
Get(Str(Last+1..10),Num2,Last);
```

will assign Num1 the value 34 and Num2 the value -23.
It is worth noting that there are subprograms for controlling the default files used when the file parameter is omitted from a text file subprogram. These are:

```
procedure Set_Input(File : in File_Type);
```
Sets the default input file to File, which must be open in the mode In_File.

```
procedure Set_Output(File : in File_Type);
```
Sets the default output file to File, which must be open in the mode Out_File.

```
function Standard_Input return File_Type;
```
Returns the standard input file.

```
function Standard_Output return File_Type;
```
Returns the standard output file.

```
function Current_Input return File_Type;
```
Returns the current default input file.

```
function Current_Output return File_Type;
```
Returns the current default file.

As an example, the procedure call:

```
Put_Line(Standard_Output,"Error - aborting program");
```

is guaranteed to print the error message to the standard output device (usually a monitor), no matter which file is the current default output file.

10.6 SEQUENTIAL FILES

There are three subprograms used for IO with sequential files: Read, Write, and End_Of_File. They are provided by the Sequential_IO package and have declarations:

```
procedure Read(File : in File_Type; Item : out Element_Type);
procedure Write(File : in File_Type; Item : in Element_Type);
function  End_Of_File(File: in File_Type) return Boolean;
```

Read and End_Of_File operate on files with mode In_File; Write operates on files of type Out_File. As an example, the following complete program creates a sequential binary file of integers that are read one per line from standard input.

```
with Text_IO; use Text_IO;
with Sequential_IO;

procedure Example is
    package Number_IO is new Sequential_IO(Integer); use Number_IO;
    package Int_IO is new Integer_IO(Integer); use Int_IO;

    Name   : String(1..20);    -- External name of sequential file.
    Length : Integer;          -- Number of characters in filename.

    F_Out : Number_IO.File_Type;  -- Sequential File variable.
    Value : Integer;              -- Reads integer from input.

begin
    Put("Enter name of integer file to create: ");
    Get_Line(Name,Length);
    Create(F_Out,Out_File,Name(1..Length));

    loop
        Put("Enter an integer (0 to quit): ");
        Get(Value);
        Skip_Line;
        exit when (Value = 0);
        Write(F_Out,Value);
      end loop;
    Close(F_Out);
end Example;
```

10.7 DIRECT-ACCESS FILES

The package `Direct_IO` provides support for direct-access files. The components of these files have a linear ordering, with their position specified by an *index*. The index of the first component is 1, with successive components having successive indexes.

An open direct-access file maintains a *current_index*, which is the index of the component used in the next read or write operation. When a file is opened, the *current_index* is 1.

For files with mode `In_File` or `Inout_File`, there are two forms of the `Read` procedure:

```
procedure Read(File : in File_Type; Item : out Element_Type);
```

and

```
procedure Read(File : in File_Type; Item : out Element_Type;
                                    From : in Positive_Count);
```

The first form reads the component, whose index is *current_index*. The second form sets the *current_index* to `From` and then reads the component with this index. In either case, the *current_index* is incremented by 1. Thus the components can be accessed in any order. For example, the call:

```
Read(RecFile,RecVar,5);
```

reads the fifth file component.

For files with mode `Inout_File` or `Out_File`, there are two forms of the `Write` procedure:

```
procedure Write(File : in File_Type; Item : in Element_Type);
```

and

```
procedure Write(File : in File_Type; Item : in Element_Type;
                                     To : in Positive_Count);
```

The first form writes the component whose index is *current_index*. The second form sets the *current_index* to `To` and then writes the component with this index. In either case, the *current_index* is incremented by 1. Thus the components can be updated in any order. For example, the call:

```
Write(RecFile,RecVar,5);
```

writes the fifth file component.

In addition to `Read` and `Write`, the following subprograms are available:

```
procedure Set_Index(File : in File_Type;
                    To : in Positive_Count);
```
Sets the *current_index* to the value of the parameter `To`. This is sometimes called a *seek* operation.

function Index(File : **in** File_Type) **return** Positive_Count;
Returns the *current_index* of the file.

function Size(File : **in** File_Type) **return** Count;
Returns the number of components in the file.

function End_Of_File(File : **in** File_Type) **return** Boolean;
Used for files open with modes In_File and Inout_File. Returns True if the *current_index* exceeds the size of the file; otherwise False is returned.

11

TASKS

11.1 INTRODUCTION

A task is an Ada program unit that can be activated and executed concurrently with other program units. Several task units can be executing, along with a main program unit. On a multiprocessor computer, this permits true parallelism within a program. On a uniprocessor computer, concurrency is achieved by interweaving the execution of tasks and the main program.

In Ada, concurrently running program units can synchronize and communicate with each other during an event called a *rendezvous*. In order for a rendezvous to occur, a task must have declared an *entry*. Entries have names and are used to specify points in the task's code where it is willing to synchronize (and perhaps communicate) with another unit. Another program unit *calls* this entry by name (in a manner analogous to a procedure call) to signal its desire to initiate a rendezvous. The *called* unit contains the entry and must be a task; the *caller* unit may be any program unit, including another task.

A rendezvous occurs only when the *caller* has made an entry call and the *called* task is at a point where it will *accept* the call. Either the *caller* or *called* unit is suspended until both conditions are satisfied, thus synchronizing the two units. Communication takes place through parameters to the entry call, just as subprograms communicate through the passing of parameters. Ada is often characterized as implementing process communication using a synchronized message-passing scheme.

A task unit is not a *compilation unit*, but rather, must be declared within a subprogram, package, or generic package. An example at the end of this chapter illustrates the declaration of a task within a package.

11.2 DECLARATION/BODY

A task unit requires both a declaration and a body. The declaration consists of a task specification in which one lists the task's entry identifiers and their parameter requirements. The body contains the executable statements. Either single tasks or task types can be declared. Task types are particularly useful. They permit the declaration of identical task objects in a manner analogous to the declaration of variables. Pointers to objects of these types (using access types) can be defined and allocators used to create and activate tasks dynamically. Task types can be passed as parameters, but the mode **out** is not allowed.

Simplified syntax for a task declaration is:

task_declaration ::= task_specification;

where

task_specification ::=

        task [type] identifier **[is**

          {entry_declaration}

        end [task_name]]

Example task declarations

```
task Writer;    -- Single tasks with no entries.
task Reader;

task Screen is                   -- A single task
   entry Display(Ch: in Character);  -- with one entry.
end Screen;

task Resource is                 -- A single task
   entry Seize;                  -- with two entries.
   entry Release;
end Resource;

task type Buffer is              -- A task type
   entry Enter(Ch: in Character);  -- with two
   entry Leave(Ch: out Character); -- entries.
end Buffer;

Keyboard      : Buffer;  -- A Buffer task.
SerialPort_In  : Buffer;  -- Another Buffer task.
SerialPort_Out : Buffer;  -- Yet another Buffer task.

type TerminalBuffers is array(1..20) of Buffer;
Terminal : TerminalBuffers;  -- An array of Buffer tasks.
```

```
type BufferPtr is access Buffer;    -- Buffer access type.

Filter : BufferPtr;    -- Variable to access a Buffer,
  ...
Filter := new Buffer;   -- Dynamically activate a
                        --   Buffer task.
```

Simplified syntax for a task body

task_body ::=

> **task body** task_name **is**
>   [declarative part]
> **begin**
>   sequence_of_statements
> **end** task_name;

Examples

```
task body Resource is
begin
  loop
     accept Seize;    -- Accept call to seize resource.
     accept Release; -- Accept call to release resource.
  end loop;
end;

task body Buffer is
     Local_Char : Character;
begin
  loop
     accept Enter(Ch : in Character) do
         Local_Char := Ch;
     end Enter;
     accept Leave(Ch : out Character) do
         Ch := Local_Char;
     end Leave;
  end loop;
end Buffer;

task body Reader is
     Char : Character;
begin
  loop
     SerialPort_In.Leave(Char); -- Rendezvous with Buffer
     Screen.Display(Char);      -- and screen tasks.
  end loop;
end Reader;
```

11.3 ENTRIES AND ACCEPT STATEMENTS

A task specification lists each entry using an *entry declaration*. Such a declaration has a syntax similar to a procedure declaration.

> entry_declaration ::=
> > **entry** identifier[(discrete_range)] [formal_part];

The optional *discrete range* declares a family of entries having the same formal part. There is one family member for each value in the discrete range. The *formal part* specifies the parameters used to pass information between the task being called and the program unit calling the task. The parameter-passage modes and their operation are the same as for procedures.

A program unit announces its desire to rendezvous with a task by making a call to an entry of the task. Syntactically, this is like a procedure call.

> entry_call_statement ::=
> > entry_name [actual_parmameter_part];

The name of an entry in an entry call is formed by taking the name of its task followed by a period, '.', followed by its identifier name.

Examples (from the previous section)

```
-- entry declarations

    entry Display(Ch : in Character); -- From Screen task.
    entry Leave(Ch : out Character);  -- From Buffer task.
    entry Release;                    -- From Resource task.

-- entry calls

    Screen.Display('r');
    SerialPort_In.Leave(Symbol);
    Terminal(3).Enter(KeyPressed);
    Filter.Leave(NewChar);
    Resource.Seize;
```

The actions to be performed during a rendezvous are specified by an accept statement in the body of the task declaring the entry. The task announces its willingness to handle an entry call by executing an accept statement.

> accept_statement ::=
> > **accept** entry_simple_name [(entry_index)] [formal_part] [**do**
> > > sequence_of_statements;
> > **end** [entry_simple_name]];

The formal part must be the same as in the entry declaration. The scope and visibility of the formal parameters are restricted to the statement sequence in the accept statement.

Examples of accept statements

```
accept Seize;        -- From the Resource task.

accept Leave(Ch : out Character) do  -- From Buffer task.
    Ch := Local_Char;
end Leave;
```

Tasks making entry calls are suspended and queued if the task containing the entry has not executed a corresponding accept statement. When an accept statement is executed, the first task in the queue participates in the rendezvous. Tasks still queued for the entry remain suspended, waiting for another execution of an accept statement.

In a similar manner, a task executing an accept statement is suspended if no other task has an active entry call for it. Thus the caller task and called task are synchronized, since one is suspended until the other is ready for the rendezvous. They are synchronized at the beginning and end of the accept statement. Thus the caller task does not proceed until the called task completes the execution of the entire accept statement.

A task such as `Resource` (in the last section) can serve to synchronize access to a shared resource. A task gains exclusive access to the resource by making the entry call:

```
Resource.Seize;
```

Having accepted this entry call, the Resource task is suspended until an entry call:

```
Resource.Release;
```

is made. In the meantime, other tasks calling `Seize` will be suspended and queued. When the task accessing the resource calls `Release`, the Resource task is no longer suspended (the rendezvous occurs), allowing a queued task to seize the resource.

The Resource task illustrates the implementation of a *semaphore* in Ada.

11.4 THE DELAY STATEMENT

A task can suspend itself by executing a **delay** statement.

delay_statement ::= **delay** simple_expression;

The value of the expression must have the predefined fixed-point type `Dura-tion`. `Duration` is declared in the standard package `Calendar` (see Appendix C). The task is suspended for at least the number of seconds specified by the expression. For example, the statement:

```
delay 0.2;
```

suspends the task that executes it for at least 0.2 seconds.

11.5 SELECT STATEMENTS

By default, a task indicating its desire to rendezvous (by executing either an accept statement or entry call) is suspended if the rendezvous cannot occur immediately. A `select` statement allows a task to indicate an alternative to being suspended.

There are three forms of select statements:

Selective Wait   allows a *called task* to accept one among several entry calls

Conditional Entry allows a *calling task* to cancel an entry call if a rendezvous cannot occur immediately

Timed Entry   allows a *calling task* to cancel an entry call if a rendezvous cannot occur within a given amount of time

Selective Waits

The syntax for a selective wait statement is:

selective_wait ::=
       select
              select_alternative
       { **or**
              select_alternative }
       [**else**
              sequence_of_statements]
       end select;

where

     select_alternative ::=
         [**when** condition =>]
                selective_wait_alternative

selective_wait_alternative ::=
      accept_alternative |
      delay_alternative |
      terminate_alternative

accept_alternative ::=
      accept_statement [sequence_of_statements]

delay_alternative ::=
      delay_statement [sequence_of_statements]

terminate_alternative ::= **terminate;**

A selective wait statement may contain several accept alternatives, but there must be at least one. In addition, it may optionally contain one, but only one, of the following:

One or more **delay** alternatives

or

A single **terminate** alternative

or

 An **else** part

Examples
Selective wait with **delay** alternative

```
-- Implementing a "screen saver" feature for the
-- Screen task of section 11.1.
    select
        accept Display(Ch: in Character) do
            Local_Char := Ch;
        end Display;
        Put(Local_Char);
    or
        delay 180.0;
        Dim_The_Screen;
    end select;
```

This select statement will wait three minutes (180 seconds) for an entry call to Display a character on the screen. If no Screen activity occurs within that time, a call is made to dim the screen.

Selective wait with `terminate` alternative

```
--   Allowing a Buffer task to terminate.

    select
        when Empty =>
            accept Enter(Ch : in Character) do
                Local_Char := Ch;
            end Enter;
            Empty := False;
    or
        when Not Empty =>
            accept Leave(Ch : out Character) do
                Ch := Local_Char;
            end Leave;
            Empty := True;
    or
        terminate;
    end select;
```

The terminate alternative is taken only when tasks using the buffer have terminated or are themselves waiting on terminate alternatives. Notice the use of **when** to control the acceptance of entry calls. The conditions following **when** are known as *guards* for the accept statements.

Selective wait with `else` part

```
-- Giving three tasks mutually exclusive access to a
-- resource without starvation or excessive waiting.

loop
    select
        when (Turn = 0) =>
            accept Seize_0;
            Turn := 1;
            Seized := True;
    or
        when (Turn = 1) =>
            accept Seize_1;
            Turn = 2;
            Seized := True;
    or
        when (Turn = 2) =>
            accept Seize_2;
            Turn := 0;
            Seized := True;
    else
        Turn := (Turn + 1) mod 3;
    end select;
    if (Seized) then
        accept Release;
        Seized := False;
```

```
        end if;
    end loop;
```

This select statement will accept an entry call to either `Seize_0`, `Seize_1`, or `Seize_2` depending on whose `Turn` it is to make an entry call. If the rendezvous cannot occur (because no task is making such an entry call), the **else** part is executed. In this example, the **else** part is used to cycle through the values of `Turn`, giving the calling tasks an opportunity to seize a shared resource.

Conditional Entry Calls

The conditional entry call allows an entry call to be canceled if a rendezvous cannot immediately occur. The syntax is:

conditional_entry_call ::=
       select
           entry_call_statement
           [sequence_of_statements]
       else
           sequence_of_statements
       end select;

If the entry call fails, the statement sequence in the **else** part is executed.

Example

```
select
    Resource.Seize;
    Put_Line("resource has been seized");
else
    Put_Line("cannot seize resource");
end select;
```

Timed Entry Calls

A timed entry call is like a conditional entry call except that the call is canceled only after a specified delay has elapsed. The syntax is:

timed_entry_call ::=
       select
           entry_call_statement
           [sequence_of_statements]
       or
           delay_alternative
       end select;

Notice that while the conditional entry call has an `else` part, the timed entry call has an `or` alternative.

Example

```
select
      Resource.Seize;
      Put_Line('resource has been seized');
or
      delay 2.0;
      Put_Line('cannot seize resource');
end select;
```

11.6 TASK ACTIVATION/DEPENDENCE/TERMINATION

If a task object declaration appears in a declarative part, it is activated after passing the reserved word `begin` immediately after the declarative part. If the task is created by the `new` allocator, it is activated at the time of allocation.

A task has a *master* on whom its existence depends. The master may be a task, block statement, subprogram, or package. A task created by the `new` allocator depends on the master containing the corresponding access type definition. Other tasks depend upon the master whose execution created them.

A task is said to be *completed* when it has finished the execution of the statements in its body.

A task becomes *terminated* if:

> It is completed and has no dependent tasks.

or

> It is completed and its dependent tasks are terminated.

or

> It has reached a terminate alternative and its master's execution is completed and tasks depending on the master are terminated or waiting on a terminate alternative.

Example

```
procedure Q is
      type BufferPtr is access Buffer;
      A, B : Buffer;
      C    : BufferPtr;
begin
      -- Activation of A and B.
      ...
      C := new Buffer;    -- Activation of C.all.
```

```
...
declare
    D : Buffer;
    E : BufferPtr := new Buffer; -- Activation of E.all.
begin
    -- Activation of D.
end;  -- Await termination of D.
end; -- Await termination of A, B, C.all, and E.all.
```

11.7 THE ABORT STATEMENT

The **abort** statement is used to terminate a task unconditionally. The syntax is:

abort_statement ::= **abort** task_name {, task_name };

Examples

```
abort  Resource, Terminal(2), SerialPort_In;
abort  Filter.all;
```

When a task is aborted, it first becomes *abnormal* and other tasks cannot rendezvous with it. An abnormal task becomes completed if it is suspended at an accept, select, or delay statement. If suspended at an entry call, the task is removed from the queue for the entry and becomes completed. If aborted prior to activation, the task is terminated. Otherwise the abnormal task does not become completed until it reaches a synchronization point such as an entry call, start or end of an accept statement, a select statement, or delay statement. A task that becomes abnormal during a rendezvous will complete the rendezvous prior to termination.

Abort statements should be used only with great care. A `Tasking_Error` exception is raised by a call to an entry of an abnormal task and is also raised in tasks suspended on a call to such an entry.

A task may abort any other task, including itself.

11.8 TASK ATTRIBUTES

Given a task T with entry E, the following attributes are defined.

T'Callable	returns the Boolean value `False` if T is completed, terminated, or abnormal, and returns `True` otherwise.
T'Terminated	returns the Boolean value `True` if T is terminated, and returns `False` otherwise.
E'Count	returns the number of entry calls queued on the entry E.

11.9 TASK EXAMPLE

The package below provides a task type for a character multiplexer. It inputs
characters from two entries and outputs them through a single entry.

```
package  MplxPkg is

   -- Task type multplx implements a 2-source to
   -- 1-destination multiplexer.

   -- Up to 128 characters are buffered. Once a source gains
   -- access to the multiplexer, it retains access until it sends
   -- the character ASCII.NUL (ascii 0).

   task type Multplx is
                  -- A family of two source entries.
      entry Mult_In(1..2)(Ch : in Character);
                  -- A single destination entry.
      entry Mult_Out(Ch : out Character);
   end MultPlx;

end MplxPkg;

package body MplxPkg is

   -- This is a 2-source multiplexer - it can easily be
   -- modified for 3, 4, or more sources.

   task body MultPlx is
      Store : array(0..127) of Character; -- Character Buffer.
      Front : Integer := 0;       -- Index of front of buffer.
      Rear  : Integer := 127;     -- Index of rear of buffer.
      Char_Count : Integer := 0;  -- Number of chars in buffer.
      Local_Char : Character;
      Turn : Integer := 1;        -- Source number that can
                                  -- store in the buffer.
      Switch_Turn : Boolean := True; -- Signals source switch.

      procedure Enter_Ch(Ch : in Character; Turn : in out Integer;
                      Switch : out Boolean) is
        -- Enter ch in the buffer, switch source if
        -- ASCII.NUL is received.
      begin
        Rear := (Rear + 1) mod 128;
        Store(Rear) := Local_Char;
        Char_Count := Char_Count + 1;
        Switch := False;
        if (ASCII.NUL = Ch) then
           Turn := (Turn mod 2 ) + 1;
           Switch := True;
        end if;
      end Enter_Ch;
```

```
begin
loop
            -- Accept input from a source.
    select
        when (Char_Count < 128) and (Turn = 1) =>
            accept Mult_In(1)(Ch : in Character) do
                Local_Char := Ch;
            end Mult_In;
            Enter_Ch(Local_Char,Turn,Switch_Turn);
    or

        when (Char_Count < 128) and (Turn = 2) =>
            accept Mult_In(2)(Ch : in Character) do
                Local_Char := Ch;
            end Mult_In;
            Enter_Ch(Local_Char,Turn,Switch_Turn);
    else
            if (Switch_Turn) then
                Turn := (Turn mod 2) + 1;
            end if;
    end select;

            -- Accept output to a destination.
    select
        when (Char_Count > 0) =>
            accept Mult_Out(Ch : out Character) do
                    Ch := Store(Front);
            end Mult_Out;
            Front := (Front+1) mod 128;
            Char_Count := Char_Count - 1;
    else
            null;
    end select;
    end loop;
  end MultPlx;
end MplxPkg;
```

To use the multiplexer, a program unit must have the **with** clause:

```
with MplxPkg;
```

A multiplexer task called Funnel is declared by:

```
Funnel : MultPlx;
```

The entry calls allowed would then be:

```
Funnel.Mult_In(1)(Char);   -- Use source 1.
Funnel.Mult_In(2)(Char);   -- Use source 2.
Funnel.Mult_Out(Char);     -- Use destination.
```

12

EXCEPTIONS

12.1 INTRODUCTION

An *exception* is an error or other abnormal condition that occurs during the execution of a program. Examples include attempts to divide by zero, index an array element with a value outside the subscript range, or open a file that does not exist. The occurrence of an exception is so catastrophic that the default action is to abort execution and (perhaps) issue an error message. Ada allows exceptions to be *handled*. This means that the program can specify code to be executed in the event of an exception. This code, called an *exception handler*, may allow the program to recover from the error or, at a minimum, print a meaningful error message and terminate the program gracefully.

When an exception occurs, it is said to be *raised*. The raising of an exception causes the program's execution to be transferred to an exception handler. If an appropriate handler does not exist, the program aborts.

This chapter covers the declaration, raising, and handling of exceptions in Ada.

12.2 PREDEFINED AND PROGRAMMER-DEFINED EXCEPTIONS

Exceptions are named. This allows different handlers to be associated with different exceptional conditions. There are five predefined exceptions. These are listed below, along with several events that cause them to be automatically raised.

Constraint_Error   raised in an attempt to access an array with an index outside the subscript range; or to access a record component that doesn't exist, given the current discriminant; or to access a dynamic variable through a **null** access variable

Numeric_Error	raised in attempting division by zero, or when an operation causes numeric overflow
Program_Error	raised in a **function** left by a means other than a **return** statement
Storage_Error	raised in evaluating an allocator (**new**) when memory space is exhausted
Tasking_Error	raised when exceptions arise during the rendezvous of tasks

There are also exceptions supplied with the standard package IO_Exceptions and used by IO packages such as Text_IO. Two of these are:

Name_Error	Raised in attempting to open a file that does not exist.
Data_Error	Raised by Get when the data item read does not have the required syntax. For example, when alphabetic characters are encountered when reading an integer.

Appendix D contains a complete listing of IO exceptions.

Ada also permits programmers to declare exceptions of their own. The syntax is:

exception_declaration ::= identifier_list : **exception**;

Examples

```
Stack_Overflow : exception;
Error, Invalid_Command : exception;
```

Exceptions, including those that are predefined, can be explicitly raised with a **raise** statement.

raise_statement ::= **raise** [exception_name];

Examples

```
raise  Stack_Overflow;
raise  Constraint_Error;
raise;  -- Allowed only within an exception handler.
```

12.3 HANDLING EXCEPTIONS

Exceptions Raised While Executing a Statement

A *frame* is a program construct that starts with the reserved word **begin** and terminates with the reserved word **end**. Frames are found in the block statement, the bodies of subprograms, packages, tasks, and generic units. Exception handlers may be placed at the end of a frame. The syntax of such a frame is:

```
begin
    sequence_of_statements
exception
    exception_handler
    { exception_handler }
end
```

Refer to the syntax of *block_statement*, *subprogram_body*, and *package_body* in the syntax summary at the back of this manual to see how they permit the handling of exceptions within their frames, using exactly this syntactic structure.

The syntax of an exception handler is:

```
exception_handler ::=
            when exception_choice {| exception_choice} =>
            sequence_of_statements
```

```
exception_choice ::= exception_name | others
```

When an exception named in an *exception_choice* occurs within a frame, execution transfers to the sequence of statements after the choice. The execution of these statements constitutes the handling of the exception; the frame's execution is complete. An **others** choice is optional, but if present, must occur last and matches all exceptions not explicitly named.

As an example, the block statement shown below handles the input of integer data in an interactive program. If invalid data is input, an exception handler prints an error message and the request for data is repeated.

```
declare
    Data_OK : Boolean;
begin
    loop                -- Prompt for integer input.
        Data_OK := True;
        Put('Enter an integer: ');
        begin
            Get(Value);
        exception
            when Data_Error =>
                Put_Line('Bad input on integer read');
                Data_Ok := False;
            when others =>
                Put_Line(' Unknown error reading data');
                Data_Ok := False;
        end;
        Skip_Line;
        exit when (Data_OK);
    end loop;
end;
```

If the frame in which an exception occurs does not contain a handler for it, the exception is said to be *propagated* to another frame. How an exception is propagated depends on the type of frame in which it is raised. If the frame is a:

subprogram	The subprogram is terminated and the same exception is raised at the point at which the subprogram was called.
block statement	The block is terminated and the same exception is raised at the point immediately after the block statement.
package body	The exception occurs during the elaboration of the package; the elaboration is terminated. If the package is a library unit, the main program is terminated; otherwise the exception is raised in the program unit containing the package body.
task	The task becomes completed.

The function shown below computes the factorial function recursively, using integer data. It contains exception handlers to handle the occurrence of a negative argument (using a locally declared exception), integer overflow, and a program error. A program error occurs if an execution of the function does not terminate with a `return` statement. If integer overflow occurs, the `Numeric_Error` exception is raised. The `Numeric_Error` exception handler in turn causes a `Program_Error` exception to be raised (can you tell why?), which in turn is propagated back through the recursive calls.

```
function Fact(n : in Integer) return Integer is
        -- Return n factorial.
    Negative : exception;
begin
    if (n < 0) then
        raise Negative;
    end if;
    if (n = 0) then
        return 1;
    else
        return n * Fact(n-1);
    end if;
exception
    when Negative =>
        Put_Line('Argument must be positive');
        return 0;
    when Numeric_Error =>
        Put(n,4);
        Put_Line('   Error - integer overflow');
    when Program_Error =>
        Put(n,4);
        Put_Line('   Program Error');
end Fact;
```

Exceptions Raised While Elaborating Declarations

An exception raised during the processing of declarations for a frame is propagated differently depending on the type of frame. In all cases, the processing of declarations halts, then, if the frame is a:

subprogram body	The exception is raised at the point of the call to the subprogram. If the subprogram is the main program, the program terminates.
block statement	The exception is raised at the point immediately following the block statement.
package body	If the package is a library unit, the main program is terminated, otherwise the exception is raised in the program unit containing the package.
task body	The task becomes completed and the exception Tasking_Error is raised at the point of the task's activation.

If the exception is raised during a package or task specification, the exception is raised in the program unit containing the specification. If the specification is a library unit, the main program is terminated.

The code segment below illustrates how an exception may occur during the elaboration of a declaration.

```
procedure Create is
    type Ptr is access Integer;
    A : Ptr := new Integer'(5);  -- May raise Storage_Error.
begin
    ...
end Create;
```

12.4 SUPPRESSING EXCEPTIONS

The **pragma** Suppress is a directive giving an Ada compiler permission to suppress various run-time checks, which in turn suppresses the raising of certain exceptions. A common example would be to suppress the check that an array index is in the valid subscript range. These run-time checks take time to perform, and they may be suppressed to increase the speed of a thoroughly debugged program. Note that the compiler is not required to obey a Suppress directive; it has only permission.

The Suppress pragma has the form:

pragma Suppress (identifier [,[On =>] name]);

The identifier denotes the run-time check to be suppressed. These affect various exceptions.

Checks affecting the exception Constraint_Error:

Access_Check	check that an access variable is not `null` when used to access a dynamic variable
Discriminant_Check	check that a record component exists for the current discriminant values
Index_Check	check that an array index is within the correct subscript range
Length_Check	check in operations involving arrays, that the arrays have the same number of elements
Range_Check	check that a value satisfies a range constraint

Checks affecting the exception `Numeric_Error`:

Division_Check	check for division by zero
Overflow_Check	check that the result of an arithmetic operation does not cause overflow

Check affecting the exception `Program_Error`:

Elaboration_Check	check that the body of a subprogram, task, or generic instantiation has been elaborated when the object is called or activated

Check affecting the exception `Storage_Error`:

Storage_Check	check that memory space is not exhausted when an allocator (**new**) is executed. Check that the space required by a subprogram call or task activation is available

The `Suppress` pragma is restricted to the declarative part of a program unit or block statement and permission to suppress a check extends only to the end of the unit or block.

The `On` option allows for the suppressing of a check to be restricted to the named object.

Examples

```
pragma Suppress (Access_Check);
pragma Suppress (Storage_Check, On => Header);
                    -- Header is an access variable.
```

A final example illustrates the use of the Suppress pragma in a procedure.

```
procedure Sort(List: in out ArrayType; Size : in Integer) is
    ...
    pragma Suppress (Index_Check);
begin
    ... Sort the array, do not check for valid subscripts.
end Sort;
```

A
ADA RESERVED WORDS[1]

abort	declare	generic	of	select
abs	delay	goto	or	separate
accept	delta		others	subtype
access	digits	if	out	
all	do	in		task
and		is	package	terminate
array			pragma	then
at	else		private	type
	elsif	limited	procedure	
	end	loop		
begin	entry		raise	use
body	exception		range	
	exit	mod	record	when
			rem	while
		new	renames	with
case	for	not	return	
constant	function	null	reverse	xor

---

1 The appendices that follow are reprinted from the *Ada Language Reference Manual* (ANSI/MIL-STD-1815A) with the permission of the Ada Joint Program office. Cross references with the appendices are for chapters and sections of the *Ada Language Reference Manual*.

B

THE PACKAGE STANDARD

```
package STANDARD is
  type BOOLEAN B is (FALSE, TRUE);

  -- The predefined relational operators for this type are as follows

  -- function "="     (LEFT, RIGHT : BOOLEAN) return BOOLEAN;
  -- function "/="    (LEFT, RIGHT : BOOLEAN) return BOOLEAN;
  -- function "<"     (LEFT, RIGHT : BOOLEAN) return BOOLEAN;
  -- function "<="    (LEFT, RIGHT : BOOLEAN) return BOOLEAN;
  -- function ">'     (LEFT, RIGHT : BOOLEAN) return BOOLEAN;
  -- function ">="    (LEFT, RIGHT : BOOLEAN) return BOOLEAN;

  -- The predefined logical operators and the predefined logical
     negation operator are as follows:

  -- function "and"  (LEFT, RIGHT : BOOLEAN) return BOOLEAN;
  -- function "or"   (LEFT, RIGHT : BOOLEAN) return BOOLEAN;
  -- function "xor"  (LEFT, RIGHT : BOOLEAN) return BOOLEAN;
  -- function "not"  (LEFT, RIGHT : BOOLEAN) return BOOLEAN;

  -- The universal type universal_integer is predefined.

  type INTEGER is implementation_ defined;
  -- The predefined operators for this type are as follows:

  -- function "="     (LEFT, RIGHT : INTEGER) return BOOLEAN;
  -- function "/="    (LEFT, RIGHT : INTEGER) return BOOLEAN;
  -- function "<"     (LEFT, RIGHT : INTEGER) return BOOLEAN;
  -- function "<="    (LEFT, RAGHT : INTEGER) return BOOLEAN;
  -- function ">"     (LEFT, RIGHT : INTEGER) return BOOLEAN;
  -- function ">="    (LEFT, RIGHT : INTEGER) return BOOLEAN;
```

```
-- function "+"    (RIGHT : INTEGER) return INTEGER;
-- function "-"    (RIGHT : INTEGER) return INTEGER;
-- function "abs"  (RIGHT : INTEGER) return INTEGER;


-- function "+"    (LEFT, RIGHT : INTEGER) return INTEGER;
-- function "-"    (LEFT, RIGHT : INTEGER) return INTEGER;
-- function "*"    (LEFT, RIGHT : INTEGER) return INTEGER;
-- function "/"    (LEFT, RIGHT : INTEGER) return INTEGER;
-- function "rem"  (LEFT, RIGHT : INTEGER) return INTEGER;
-- function "mod"  (LEFT, RIGHT : INTEGER) return INTEGER;


-- function "**"   (LEFT : INTEGER; RIGHT : INTEGER) return INTEGER;
```

-- An implementation may provide additional predefined integer
-- types. It is recommended that the names of such additional types
-- end with INTEGER, as in SHORT_INTEGER or LONG_INTEGER. The
-- specification of each operator for the type *universal_integer*,
-- or for any additional predefined integer type, is obtained by
-- replacing INTEGER with the name of the type in the specification
-- of the corresponding operator of the type INTEGER, except for
-- the right operand of the exponentiating operator.

-- The universal type *universal_real* is predefined.

type FLOAT **is** *implementation_defined*;

-- The predefined operators for this type are as follows:

```
-- function "="    (LEFT, RIGHT : FLOAT) return BOOLEAN;
-- function "/="   (LEFT, RIGHT : FLOAT) return BOOLEAN;
-- function "<"    (LEFT, RIGHT : FLOAT) return BOOLEAN;
-- function "<="   (LEFT, RIGHT : FLOAT) return BOOLEAN;
-- function ">"    (LEFT, RIGHT : FLOAT) return BOOLEAN;
-- function ">="   (LEFT, RIGHT : FLOAT) return BOOLEAN;


-- function "+"    (RIGHT : FLOAT) return FLOAT;
-- function "-"    (RIGHT : FLOAT) return FLOAT;
-- function "abs"  (RIGHT : FLOAT) return FLOAT;


-- function "+"    (LEFT, RIGHT : FLOAT) return FLOAT;
-- function "-"    (LEFT, RIGHT : FLOAT) return FLOAT;
-- function "*"    (LEFT, RIGHT : FLOAT) return FLOAT;
-- function "/"    (LEFT, RIGHT : FLOAT) return FLOAT;


-- function "**"   (LEFT : FLOAT; RIGHT : INTEGER) return FLOAT;
```

-- An implementation may provide additional predefined floating-
-- point types. It is recommended that the names of such
-- additional types end with FLOAT, as in SHORT_FLOAT or
-- LONG_FLOAT. The specification of each operator for the type
-- *universal_real*, or for any additional predefined floating-

```
-- point type, is obtained by replacing FLOAT with the name of the
-- type in the specification of the corresponding operator of the
-- type FLOAT.
-- In addition, the following operators are predefined for
-- universal types.

-- function "*"  (LEFT : universal_integer;
                  RIGHT : universal_real) return universal_real;
-- function "*"  (LEFT : universal_real;
                  RIGHT : universal_integer) return universal_real;
-- function "/"  (LEFT : universal_real;
                  RIGHT : universal_integer) return universal_real;

-- The type universal_fixed is predefined.  The only operators
-- declared for this type are:

-- function "*"  (LEFT : any_fixed_point_type;
                  RIGHT : any_fixed_point_type) return universal_fixed;
-- function "/"  (LEFT : any_fixed_point_type;
                  RIGHT : any_fixed_point_type) return universal_fixed;

-- The following characters form the standard ASCII character set.
-- Character literals corresponding to control characters are not
-- identifiers; they are indicated in italics in this definition.

type CHARACTER is
( nul,   soh,   stx,   etx,      eot,   enq,   ack,   bel,
  bs,    ht,    lf,    vt,       ff,    cr,    so,    si,
  dle,   dc1,   dc2,   dc3,      dc4,   nak,   syn,   etb,
  can,   em,    sub,   esc,      fs,    gs,    rs,    us,

  ' ',   '!',   '"',   '#',      '$',   '%',   '&',   ''',
  '(',   ')',   '*',   '+',      ',',   '-',   '.',   '/',
  '0',   '1',   '2',   '3',      '4',   '5',   '6',   '7',
  '8',   '9',   ':',   ';',      '<',   '=',   '>',   '?',

  '@',   'A',   'B',   'C',      'D',   'E',   'F',   'G',
  'H',   'I',   'J',   'K',      'L',   'M',   'N',   'O',
  'P',   'Q',   'R',   'S',      'T',   'U',   'V',   'W',
  'X',   'Y',   'Z',   '[',      '\',   ']',   '^',   '_',

  ''',   'a',   'b',   'c',      'd',   'e',   'f',   'g',
  'h',   'i',   'j',   'k',      'l',   'm',   'n',   'o',
  'p',   'q',   'r',   's',      't',   'u',   'v',   'w',
  'x',   'y',   'z',   '{',      '|',   '}',   '~',   del,

for CHARACTER use  -- 128 ASCII character set without holes
     (0, 1, 2, 3, 4, 5, ..., 125, 126, 127);

-- The predefined operators for the type CHARACTER are the same
-- as for any enumeration type.
```

```
package ASCII is

   -- Control Characters:

   NUL : constant CHARACTER := nul;    SOH : constant CHARACTER := soh;
   STX : constant CHARACTER := stx;    ETX : constant CHARACTER := etx;
   EOT : constant CHARACTER := eot;    ENQ : constant CHARACTER := enq;
   ACK : constant CHARACTER := ack;    BEL : constant CHARACTER := bel;
   BS  : constant CHARACTER := bs;     HT  : constant CHARACTER := ht;
   LF  : constant CHARACTER := lf;     VT  : constant CHARACTER := vt;
   FF  : constant CHARACTER := ff;     CR  : constant CHARACTER := cr;
   SO  : constant CHARACTER := so;     SI  : constant CHARACTER := si;
   DLE : constant CHARACTER := dle;    DC1 : constant CHARACTER := dc1;
   DC2 : constant CHARACTER := dc2;    DC3 : constant CHARACTER := dc3;
   DC4 : constant CHARACTER := dc4;    NAK : constant CHARACTER := nak;
   SYN : constant CHARACTER := syn;    ETB : constant CHARACTER := etb;
   CAN : constant CHARACTER := can;    EM  : constant CHARACTER := em;
   SUB : constant CHARACTER := sub;    ESC : constant CHARACTER := esc;
   FS  : constant CHARACTER := fs;     GS  : constant CHARACTER := gs;
   RS  : constant CHARACTER := rs;     US  : constant CHARACTER := us;
   DEL : constant CHARACTER := del;

   -- Other Characters:

   EXCLAM      : constant CHARACTER :='!';
   SHARP       : constant CHARACTER :='#';
   PERCENT     : constant CHARACTER :='%';
   COLON       : constant CHARACTER :=':';
   QUERY       : constant CHARACTER :='?';
   L_BRACKET   : constant CHARACTER :='[';
   R_BRACKET   : constant CHARACTER :=']';
   UNDERLINE   : constant CHARACTER :='_';
   L_BRACE     : constant CHARACTER :='{';
   R_BRACE     : constant CHARACTER :='}';
   QUOTATION   : constant CHARACTER :='"';
   DOLLAR      : constant CHARACTER :='$';
   AMPERSAND   : constant CHARACTER :='&';
   SEMICOLON   : constant CHARACTER :=';';
   AT_SIGN     : constant CHARACTER :='@';
   BACK_SLASH  : constant CHARACTER :='\';
   CIRCUMFLEX  : constant CHARACTER :='^';
   GRAVE       : constant CHARACTER :='`';
   BAR         : constant CHARACTER :='|';
   TILDE       : constant CHARACTER :='~';

   -- Lowercase letters:

   LC_A : constant CHARACTER := 'a';
   ...
   LC_Z : constant CHARACTER := 'z';

end ASCII;
```

```
-- Predefined Subtypes

subtype NATURAL is INTEGER range 0 .. INTEGER'LAST;
subtype POSITIVE is INTEGER range 1 .. INTEGER'LAST;
-- Predefined String Type:

type STRING is array(POSITIVE range <>) of CHARACTER;

pragma PACK(STRING);

-- The predefined operators of this type are as follows:

-- function "="   (LEFT, RIGHT : STRING) return BOOLEAN;
-- function "/="  (LEFT, RIGHT : STRING) return BOOLEAN;
-- function "<"   (LEFT, RIGHT : STRING) return BOOLEAN;
-- function "<="  (LEFT, RIGHT : STRING) return BOOLEAN;
-- function ">"   (LEFT, RIGHT : STRING) return BOOLEAN;
-- function ">="  (LEFT, RIGHT : STRING) return BOOLEAN;
-- function "&"  (LEFT : STRING;    RIGHT : STRING) return STRING;
-- function "&"  (LEFT : CHARACTER; RIGHT : STRING) return STRING;
-- function "&"  (LEFT : STRING;    RIGHT : CHARACTER) return STRING;
-- function "&"  (LEFT : CHARACTER; RIGHT : CHARACTER) return STRING;

type DURATION is
          delta implementation_defined range implementation_defined;

-- The predefined operators for the type DURATION are the same as for
-- any fixed-point type.

-- The Predefined Exceptions:

CONSTRAINT_ERROR : exception;
NUMERIC_ERROR    : exception;
PROGRAM_ERROR    : exception;
STORAGE_ERROR    : exception;
TASKING_ERROR    : exception;
```

C

THE PACKAGE CALENDAR

```ada
package CALENDAR is
    type TIME is private

    subtype YEAR_NUMBER is INTEGER range 1901 ..2099;
    subtype MONTH_NUMBER is INTEGER range 1 .. 12;
    subtype DAY_NUMBER is INTEGER range 1 ..31;
    subtype DAY_DURATION is DURATION range 0.0 .. 86_400.0;

    function CLOCK return TIME;

    function YEAR (DATE : TIME) return YEAR_NUMBER;
    function MONTH (DATE : TIME) return MONTH_NUMBER;
    function DAY (DATE : TIME) return DAY_NUMBER;

    procedure SPLIT ( DATE      : in TIME;
                      YEAR      : out YEAR_NUMBER;
                      MONTH     : out MONTH_NUMBER;
                      DAY       : out DAY_NUMBER;
                      SECONDS   : out DAY_DURATION);

    function TIME_OF( YEAR      : YEAR_NUMBER;
                      MONTH     : MONTH_NUMBER;
                      DAY       : DAY_NUMBER;
                      SECONDS   : DAY_DURATION := 0.0) return TIME;
    function "+" (LEFT : TIME;     RIGHT : DURATION) return TIME;
    function "+" (LEFT : DURATION; RIGHT : TIME)     return TIME;
    function "-" (LEFT : TIME;     RIGHT : DURATION) return TIME;
    function "-" (LEFT : TIME;     RIGHT : TIME)     return DURATION;

    function "<"  (LEFT, RIGHT : DURATION) return BOOLEAN;
    function "<=" (LEFT, RIGHT : DURATION) return BOOLEAN;
    function ">"  (LEFT, RIGHT : DURATION) return BOOLEAN;
    function ">=" (LEFT, RIGHT : DURATION) return BOOLEAN;
```

```
    TIME_ERROR : exception; -- Can be raised by TIME_OF, "+", and '-'.

private
    -- Implementation-dependent.
end;
```

D

THE PACKAGE
IO_EXCEPTIONS

```
package IO_EXCEPTIONS is
      STATUS_ERROR   : exception;
      MODE_ERROR     : exception;
      NAME_ERROR     : exception;
      USE_ERROR      : exception;
      DEVICE_ERROR   : exception;
      END_ERROR      : exception;
      DATA_ERROR     : exception;
      LAYOUT_ERROR   : exception;
end IO_EXCEPTIONS;
```

THE PACKAGE SYSTEM

```
package SYSTEM is

    type ADDRESS is implementation_defined;
    type NAME    is implementation_defined_enumeration_type;

    SYSTEM_NAME     : constant NAME := implementation_defined;
    STORAGE_UNIT    : constant := implementation_defined;
    MEMORY_SIZE     : constant := implementation_defined;

-- System-dependent Named Numbers:

    MIN_INT         : constant := implementation_defined;
    MAX_INT         : constant := implementation_defined;
    MAX_DIGITS      : constant := implementation_defined;
    MAX_MANTISSA    : constant := implementation_defined;
    FINE_DELTA      : constant := implementation_defined;
    TICK            : constant := implementation_defined;

-- Other System-dependent Declarations

    subtype PRIORITY is INTEGER range implementation_defined;

    ...
end SYSTEM;
```

3

THE PACKAGE SYSTEM

THE PACKAGE
SEQUENTIAL_IO

```
with IO_EXCEPTIONS;
generic
    type ELEMENT_TYPE is private;
package SEQUENTIAL_IO is

    type FILE-TYPE is limited private;
    type FILE_MODE is (IN_FILE, OUT_FILE);

    -- File Management

    procedure CREATE( FILE  : in out FILE_TYPE;
                      MODE  : in FILE_MODE := OUT_FILE;
                      NAME  : in STRING := "";
                      FORM  : in STRING := "");

    procedure OPEN  ( FILE  : in out FILE_TYPE;
                      MODE  : in FILE_MODE;
                      NAME  : in STRING;
                      FORM  : in STRING := "");

    procedure CLOSE  (FILE : in out FILE_TYPE);
    procedure DELETE (FILE : in out FILE_TYPE);
    procedure RESET  (FILE : in out FILE_TYPE; MODE : in FILE_MODE);
    procedure RESET  (FILE : in out FILE_TYPE);
    function MODE  (FILE : in FILE_TYPE) return FILE_MODE;
    function NAME  (FILE : in FILE_TYPE) return STRING;
    function FORM  (FILE : in FILE_TYPE) return STRING;

    function IS_OPEN (FILE : in FILE_TYPE) return BOOLEAN;
```

```
-- Input and Output Operations

procedure READ  (FILE : in FILE_TYPE; ITEM : out ELEMENT_TYPE);
procedure WRITE (FILE : in FILE_TYPE; ITEM : in ELEMENT_TYPE);

function END_OF_FILE(FILE : in FILE_TYPE) return BOOLEAN;

-- Exceptions:

STATUS_ERROR : exception renames IO_EXCEPTIONS.STATUS_ERROR;
MODE_ERROR   : exception renames IO_EXCEPTIONS.MODE_ERROR;
NAME_ERROR   : exception renames IO_EXCEPTIONS.NAME_ERROR;
USE_ERROR    : exception renames IO_EXCEPTIONS.USE_ERROR;
DEVICE_ERROR : exception renames IO_EXCEPTIONS.DEVICE_ERROR;
END_ERROR    : exception renames IO_EXCEPTIONS.END_ERROR;
DATA_ERROR   : exception renames IO_EXCEPTIONS.DATA_ERROR;

private
     -- Implementation-dependent:
end SEQUENTIAL_IO;
```

G

THE PACKAGE DIRECT_IO

```
with IO_EXCEPTIONS;
generic
     type ELEMENT_TYPE is private;
package DIRECT_IO is

     type FILE-TYPE is limited private;

     type FILE_MODE is (IN_FILE, INOUT_FILE, OUT_FILE);
     type COUNT      is range 0 .. implementation_defined;
     subtype POSITIVE_COUNT is COUNT range 1 .. COUNT'LAST;

     -- File Management:

     procedure CREATE( FILE : in out FILE_TYPE;
                       MODE : in FILE_MODE := INOUT_FILE;
                       NAME : in STRING := "";
                       FORM : in STRING := "");

     procedure OPEN  ( FILE : in out FILE_TYPE;
                       MODE : in FILE_MODE;
                       NAME : in STRING;
                       FORM : in STRING := "");

     procedure CLOSE  (FILE : in out FILE_TYPE);
     procedure DELETE (FILE : in out FILE_TYPE);
     procedure RESET  (FILE : in out FILE_TYPE; MODE : in FILE_MODE);
     procedure RESET  (FILE : in out FILE_TYPE);

     function MODE  (FILE : in FILE_TYPE) return FILE_MODE;
     function NAME  (FILE : in FILE_TYPE) return STRING;
     function FORM  (FILE : in FILE_TYPE) return STRING;

     function IS_OPEN (FILE : in FILE_TYPE) return BOOLEAN;
```

```
-- Input and Output Operations:

procedure READ  (FILE : in FILE_TYPE;
                 ITEM : out ELEMENT_TYPE;
                 FROM : POSITIVE_COUNT);
procedure READ  (FILE : in FILE_TYPE; ITEM : out ELEMENT_TYPE);

procedure WRITE (FILE : in FILE_TYPE;
                 ITEM : in ELEMENT_TYPE;
                 TO   : POSITIVE_COUNT);
procedure WRITE (FILE : in FILE_TYPE; ITEM : in ELEMENT_TYPE);

procedure SET_INDEX(FILE : in FILE_TYPE; TO : in POSITIVE_COUNT);

function INDEX(FILE : in FILE_TYPE) return POSITIVE_COUNT;
function SIZE (FILE : in FILE_TYPE) return COUNT;
function END_OF_FILE(FILE : in FILE_TYPE) return BOOLEAN;

-- Exceptions:

STATUS_ERROR : exception renames IO_EXCEPTIONS.STATUS_ERROR;
MODE_ERROR   : exception renames IO_EXCEPTIONS.MODE_ERROR;
NAME_ERROR   : exception renames IO_EXCEPTIONS.NAME_ERROR;
USE_ERROR    : exception renames IO_EXCEPTIONS.USE_ERROR;
DEVICE_ERROR : exception renames IO_EXCEPTIONS.DEVICE_ERROR;
END_ERROR    : exception renames IO_EXCEPTIONS.END_ERROR;
DATA_ERROR   : exception renames IO_EXCEPTIONS.DATA_ERROR;

private
-- Implementation-dependent:
end DIRECT_IO;
```

THE PACKAGE
TEXT_IO

```
with IO_EXCEPTIONS;
package DIRECT_IO is

   type FILE-TYPE is limited private;
   type FILE_MODE is (IN_FILE, OUT_FILE);
   type COUNT      is range 0 .. implementation_defined;
   subtype POSITIVE_COUNT is COUNT range 1 .. COUNT'LAST;
   UNBOUNDED : constant COUNT := 0; -- Line and page length.

   subtype FIELD       is INTEGER range 0 .. implementation_defined;
   subtype NUMBER_BASE is INTEGER range 2 .. 16;

   type TYPE_SET is (LOWER_CASE, UPPER_CASE);

   -- File Management:

   procedure CREATE( FILE  : in out FILE_TYPE;
                     MODE  : in FILE_MODE := OUT_FILE;
                     NAME  : in STRING := "";
                     FORM  : in STRING := "");

   procedure OPEN  ( FILE  : in out FILE_TYPE;
                     MODE  : in FILE_MODE;
                     NAME  : in STRING;
                     FORM  : in STRING := "");

   procedure CLOSE  (FILE : in out FILE_TYPE);
   procedure DELETE (FILE : in out FILE_TYPE);
   procedure RESET  (FILE : in out FILE_TYPE; MODE : in FILE_MODE);
   procedure RESET  (FILE : in out FILE_TYPE);

   function MODE  (FILE : in FILE_TYPE) return FILE_MODE;
   function NAME  (FILE : in FILE_TYPE) return STRING;
```

```
function FORM  (FILE : in FILE_TYPE) return STRING;

function IS_OPEN (FILE : in FILE_TYPE) return BOOLEAN;

-- Control of Default Input and Output Files:

procedure SET_INPUT  (FILE : in FILE_TYPE);
procedure SET_OUTPUT (FILE : in FILE_TYPE);

function STANDARD_INPUT  return FILE_TYPE;
function STANDARD_OUTPUT return FILE_TYPE;

function CURRENT_INPUT   return FILE_TYPE;
function CURRENT_OUTPUT  return FILE_TYPE;

procedure SET_LINE_LENGTH (FILE : in FILE_TYPE; TO : in COUNT);
procedure SET_LINE_LENGTH (TO : in COUNT);

procedure SET_PAGE_LENGTH(FILE : in FILE_TYPE; TO : in COUNT);
procedure SET_PAGE_LENGTH(TO : in COUNT);

function LINE_LENGTH (FILE : in FILE_TYPE) return COUNT;
function LINE_LENGTH  return COUNT;

function PAGE_LENGTH (FILE : in FILE_TYPE) return COUNT;
function PAGE_LENGTH  return COUNT;

-- Column, Line, and Page Control:

procedure NEW_LINE (FILE : in FILE_TYPE;
                    SPACING : in POSITIVE_COUNT := 1);
procedure NEW_LINE (SPACING : in POSITIVE_COUNT := 1);

procedure SKIP_LINE (FILE : in FILE_TYPE;
                     SPACING : in POSITIVE_COUNT := 1);
procedure SKIP_LINE (SPACING : in POSITIVE_COUNT := 1);

function END_OF_LINE (FILE : in FILE_TYPE) return BOOLEAN;
function END_OF_LINE  return BOOLEAN;

procedure NEW_PAGE (FILE : in FILE_TYPE);
procedure NEW_PAGE;

procedure SKIP_PAGE (FILE : in FILE_TYPE);
procedure SKIP_PAGE;

function END_OF_PAGE (FILE : in FILE_TYPE) return BOOLEAN;
function END_OF_PAGE  return BOOLEAN;

function END_OF_FILE (FILE : in FILE_TYPE) return BOOLEAN;
function END_OF_FILE  return BOOLEAN;
```

```
procedure SET_COL (FILE : in FILE_TYPE; TO : in POSITIVE_COUNT);
procedure SET_COL (TO : in POSITIVE_COUNT);

procedure SET_LINE(FILE : in FILE_TYPE; TO : in POSITIVE_COUNT);
procedure SET_LINE(TO : in POSITIVE_COUNT);

function COL (FILE : in FILE_TYPE)  return POSITIVE_COUNT;
function COL  return POSITIVE_COUNT;

function LINE (FILE : in FILE_TYPE)  return POSITIVE_COUNT;
function LINE  return POSITIVE_COUNT;

function PAGE (FILE : in FILE_TYPE)  return POSITIVE_COUNT;
function PAGE  return POSITIVE_COUNT;

-- Character Input-Output:

procedure GET(FILE : in FILE_TYPE; ITEM : out CHARACTER);
procedure GET(ITEM : out CHARACTER);
procedure PUT(FILE : in FILE_TYPE; ITEM : in CHARACTER);
procedure PUT(ITEM : in CHARACTER);

-- String Input-Output:

procedure GET(FILE : in FILE_TYPE; ITEM : out STRING);
procedure GET(ITEM : out STRING);
procedure PUT(FILE : in FILE_TYPE; ITEM : in STRING);
procedure PUT(ITEM : in STRING);

procedure GET_LINE(FILE : in FILE_TYPE; ITEM : out STRING;
                                        LAST : out NATURAL);
procedure GET_LINE(ITEM : out STRING; LAST : out NATURAL);
procedure PUT_LINE(FILE : in FILE_TYPE; ITEM : in STRING);
procedure PUT_LINE(ITEM : in STRING);

-- Generic Package for Input-Output of Integer Types:

generic
   type NUM IS range <>;
package INTEGER_IO is

   DEFAULT_WIDTH : FIELD := NUM'WIDTH;
   DEFAULT_BASE  : NUMBER_BASE := 10;

   procedure GET(FILE : in FILE_TYPE;
                 ITEM : out NUM; WIDTH : in FIELD := 0);
   procedure GET(ITEM : out NUM; WIDTH : in FIELD := 0);

   procedure PUT(FILE  : in FILE_TYPE;
                 ITEM  : in NUM;
                 WIDTH : in FIELD := DEFAULT_WIDTH;
                 BASE  : in NUMBER_BASE := DEFAULT_BASE);
```

```
   procedure PUT(ITEM  : in NUM;
                 WIDTH : in FIELD := DEFAULT_WIDTH;
                 BASE  : in NUMBER_BASE := DEFAULT_BASE);

   procedure GET(FROM : in STRING;
                 ITEM : out NUM; LAST : out POSITIVE);

   procedure PUT(TO    : out STRING;
                 ITEM  : in NUM;
                 BASE  : in NUMBER_BASE := DEFAULT_BASE);

end INTEGER_IO;

-- Generic Packages for Input-Output of Real Types:

generic
   type NUM is digits <>;
package FLOAT_IO is;

   DEFAULT_FORE : FIELD := 2;
   DEFAULT_AFT  : FIELD := NUM'DIGITS-1;
   DEFAULT_EXP  : FIELD := 3;

   procedure GET(FILE : in FILE_TYPE;
                 ITEM : out NUM; WIDTH : in FIELD := 0);
   procedure GET(ITEM : out NUM; WIDTH : in FIELD := 0);

   procedure PUT(FILE : in FILE_TYPE;
                 ITEM : in NUM;
                 FORE : in FIELD := DEFAULT_FORE;
                 AFT  : in FIELD := DEFAULT_AFT;
                 EXP  : in FIELD := DEFAULT_EXP);
   procedure PUT(ITEM : in NUM;
                 FORE : in FIELD := DEFAULT_FORE;
                 AFT  : in FIELD := DEFAULT_AFT;
                 EXP  : in FIELD := DEFAULT_EXP);

   procedure GET(FROM : in STRING;
                 ITEM : out NUM; LAST : out POSITIVE);
   procedure PUT(TO   : out STRING;
                 ITEM : in NUM;
                 AFT  : in FIELD := DEFAULT_AFT;
                 EXP  : in FIELD := DEFAULT_EXP);

end FLOAT_IO;


generic
   type NUM is delta <>;
package FIXED_IO is;
```

```
      DEFAULT_FORE : FIELD := NUM'FORE;
      DEFAULT_AFT  : FIELD := NUM'AFT;
      DEFAULT_EXP  : FIELD := 0;
      procedure GET(FILE : in FILE_TYPE;
                    ITEM : out NUM; WIDTH : in FIELD := 0);
      procedure GET(ITEM : out NUM; WIDTH : in FIELD := 0);

      procedure PUT(FILE : in FILE_TYPE;
                    ITEM : in NUM;
                    FORE : in FIELD := DEFAULT_FORE;
                    AFT  : in FIELD := DEFAULT_AFT;
                    EXP  : in FIELD := DEFAULT_EXP);
      procedure PUT(ITEM : in NUM;
                    FORE : in FIELD := DEFAULT_FORE;
                    AFT  : in FIELD := DEFAULT_AFT;
                    EXP  : in FIELD := DEFAULT_EXP);

      procedure GET(FROM : in STRING;
                    ITEM : out NUM; LAST : out POSITIVE);
      procedure PUT(TO   : out STRING;
                    ITEM : in NUM;
                    AFT  : in FIELD := DEFAULT_AFT;
                    EXP  : in FIELD := DEFAULT_EXP);
  end FIXED_IO;

-- Generic Package for Input-Output of Enumeration Types:


generic
   type ENUM is  (<>);
package ENUMERATION_IO is;

   DEFAULT_WIDTH   : FIELD := 0;
   DEFAULT_SETTING : TYPE_SET := UPPER_CASE;

   procedure GET(FILE : in FILE_TYPE; ITEM : out ENUM);
   procedure GET(ITEM : out ENUM);

   procedure PUT(FILE  : in FILE_TYPE;
                 ITEM  : in ENUM;
                 WIDTH : in FIELD    := DEFAULT_WIDTH;
                 SET   : in TYPE_SET := DEFAULT_SETTING);
   procedure PUT(ITEM  : in ENUM;
                 WIDTH : in FIELD    := DEFAULT_WIDTH;
                 SET   : in TYPE_SET := DEFAULT_SETTING);

   procedure GET(FROM : in STRING;
                 ITEM : out ENUM; LAST : out POSITIVE);
   procedure PUT(TO   : out STRING;
                 ITEM : in ENUM;
                 SET  : in TYPE_SET := DEFAULT_SETTING);
end ENUMERATION_IO;
```

```
    -- Exceptions:

    STATUS_ERROR  : exception renames IO_EXCEPTIONS.STATUS_ERROR;
    MODE_ERROR    : exception renames IO_EXCEPTIONS.MODE_ERROR;
    NAME_ERROR    : exception renames IO_EXCEPTIONS.NAME_ERROR;
    USE_ERROR     : exception renames IO_EXCEPTIONS.USE_ERROR;
    DEVICE_ERROR  : exception renames IO_EXCEPTIONS.DEVICE_ERROR;
    END_ERROR     : exception renames IO_EXCEPTIONS.END_ERROR;
    DATA_ERROR    : exception renames IO_EXCEPTIONS.DATA_ERROR;
    LAYOUT_ERROR  : exception renames IO_EXCEPTIONS.LAYOUT_ERROR;

private
    -- Implementation-dependent.
end TEXT_IO;
```

I
ATTRIBUTES

This annex summarizes the definitions given elsewhere of the predefined language attributes.

P'ADDRESS   For a prefix P that denotes an object, a program unit, a label, or an entry:

Yields the address of the first of the storage units allocated to P. For a subprogram, package, task unit, or label, this value refers to the machine code associated with the corresponding body or statement. For an entry for which an address clause has been given, the value refers to the corresponding hardware interrupt. The value of this attribute is of the type ADDRESS defined in the package SYSTEM. (See 13.7.2.)[1]

P'AFT   For a prefix P that denotes a fixed-point subtype:

Yields the number of decimal digits needed after the point to accommodate the precision of the subtype P, unless the delta of the subtype P is greater than 0.1, in which case the attribute yields the value one. (P'AFT is the smallest positive integer N for which (10**N)*P'DELTA is greater than or equal to one.) The value of this attribute is of the type *universal_integer*. (See 3.5.10.)

P'BASE   For a prefix P that denotes a type or subtype:

This attribute denotes the base type of P. It is allowed only as the prefix of the name of another attribute: for example, P'BASE'FIRST. (See 3.3.3.)

P'CALLABLE   For a prefix P that is appropriate for a task type:

Yields the value FALSE when the execution of the task P is either completed or terminated, or when the task is abnormal; yields the value TRUE otherwise. The value of this attribute is of the predefined type BOOLEAN. (See 9.9.)

---

1 Cross references are for chapters and sections of the *Ada Language Reference Manual*; see note Appendix A.

P'CONSTRAINED   For a prefix P that denotes an object of a type with discriminants:

Yields the value TRUE if a discriminant constraint applies to the object P, or if the object is a constant (including a formal parameter or generic formal parameter of mode **in**); yields the value FALSE otherwise. If P is a generic formal parameter of mode **in out**, or if P is a formal parameter of mode **in out** or **out** and the type mark given in the corresponding parameter specification denotes an unconstrained type with discriminants, then the value of this attribute is obtained from that of the corresponding actual parameter. The value of this attribute is of the predefined type BOOLEAN. (See 3.7.4.)

P'CONSTRAINED   For a prefix P that denotes a private type or subtype:

Yields the value FALSE if P denotes an unconstrained nonformal private type with discriminants; also yields the value FALSE if P denotes a generic formal private type and the associated actual subtype is either an unconstrained type with discriminants or an unconstrained array type; yields the value TRUE otherwise. The value of this attribute is of the predefined type BOOLEAN. (See 7.4.2.)

P'COUNT   For a prefix P that denotes an entry of a task unit:

Yields the number of entry calls presently queued on the entry (if the attribute is evaluated within an accept statement for the entry P, the count does not include the calling task). The value of this attribute is of the type *universal_integer*. (See 9.9.)

P'DELTA   For a prefix P that denotes a fixed-point subtype:

Yields the value of the delta specified in the fixed accuracy definition for the subtype P. The value of this attribute is of the type *universal_real*. (See 3.5.10.)

P'DIGITS   For a prefix P that denotes a floating point subtype:

Yields the number of decimal digits in the decimal mantissa of model numbers of the subtype P. (This attribute yields the number D of section 3.5.7.) The value of this attribute is of the type *universal_integer*. (See 3.5.8.)

P'EMAX   For a prefix P that denotes a floating-point subtype:

Yields the largest exponent value in the binary canonical form of model numbers of the subtype P. (This attribute yields the product 4*B of section 3.5.7.) The value of this attribute is of the type *universal_integer*. (See 3.5.8.)

P'EPSILON   For a prefix P that denotes a floating point subtype:

Yields the absolute value of the difference between the model number 1.0 and the next model number above, for the subtype P. The value of this attribute is of the type *universal_real*. (See 3.5.8.)

P'FIRST   For a prefix P that denotes a scalar type, or a subtype
                     of a scalar type:

Yields the lower bound of P. The value of this attribute has the same type
as P. (See 3.5.)

P'FIRST   For a prefix P that is appropriate for an array type, or
                     that denotes a constrained array subtype:

Yields the lower bound of the first index range. The value of this attribute
has the same type as this lower bound. (See 3.6.2 and 3.8.2.)

P'FIRST(N)   For a prefix P that is appropriate for an array type, or
                     that denotes a constrained array subtype:

Yields the lower bound of the N-th index range. The value of this attribute
has the same type as this lower bound. The argument N must be a static expression of type *universal_integer*. The value of N must be positive (nonzero) and no
greater than the dimensionality of the array. (See 3.6.2 and 3.8.2.)

P'FIRST_BIT   For a prefix P that denotes a component of a record
                     object:

Yields the offset, from the start of the first storage units occupied by the
component, to the first bit occupied by the component. This offset is measured
in bits. The value of this attribute is of the type *universal_integer*. (See 13.7.2.)

P'FORE   For a prefix P that denotes a fixed-point subtype:

Yields the minimum number of characters needed for the integer part of
the decimal representation of any value of the subtype P, assuming that the representation does not include an exponent, but includes a one-character prefix
that is either a minus sign or a space. (This minimum number does not include
superfluous zeros or underlines, and is at least two.) The value of this attribute
is of the type *universal_integer*. (See 3.5.10.)

P'IMAGE   For a prefix P that denotes a discrete type or subtype:

This attribute is a function with a single parameter. The actual parameter
X must be a value of the base type P. The result type is the predefined type
STRING. The result is the *image* of the value of X, that is, a sequence of characters representing the value in display form. The image of an integer value is the
corresponding decimal literal; without underlines, leading zeros, exponent, or
trailing spaces, but with a one-character prefix that is either a minus sign or a
space.

The image of an enumeration value is either the corresponding identifier
in uppercase or the corresponding character literal (including the two apostrophes); neither leading nor trailing spaces are included. The image of a character
other than a graphic character is implementation defined. (See 3.5.5.)

P'LARGE   For a prefix P that denotes a real subtype:

The attribute yields the largest positive model number of the subtype P. The value of this attribute is of the type *universal_real*. (See 3.5.8 and 3.5.10.)

P'LAST   For a prefix P that denotes a scalar type, or a subtype of a scalar type:

Yields the upper bound of P. The value of this attribute has the same type as P. (See 3.5.)

P'LAST   For a prefix P that is appropriate for an array type, or that denotes a constrained array subtype:

Yields the upper bound of the first index range. The value of this attribute has the same type as this upper bound. (See 3.6.2 and 3.8.2.)

P'LAST(N)   For a prefix P that is appropriate for an array type, or that denotes a constrained array subtype:

Yields the upper bound of the N-th index range. The value of this attribute has the same type as this upper bound. The argument N must be a static expression of type *universal_integer*. The value of N must be positive (nonzero) and no greater than the dimensionality of the array. (See 3.6.2 and 3.8.2.)

P'LAST_BIT   For a prefix P that denotes a component of a record object:

Yields the offset, from the start of the first storage units occupied by the component, to the last bit occupied by the component. This offset is measured in bits. The value of this attribute is of the type *universal_integer*. (See 13.7.2.)

P'LENGTH   For a prefix P that is appropriate for an array type, or that denotes a constrained array subtype:

Yields the number of values of the first index range (zero for a null range). The value of this attribute is of the type *universal_integer*. (See 3.6.2.)

P'LENGTH(N)   For a prefix P that is appropriate for an array type, or that denotes a constrained array subtype:

Yields the number of values of the N-th index range (zero for a null range). The value of this attribute is of the type *universal_integer*. The argument N must be a static expression of type *universal_integer*. The value of N must be positive (nonzero) and no greater than the dimensionality of the array. (See 3.6.2 and 3.8.2.)

P'MACHINE_EMAX   For a prefix P that denotes a floating point type or subtype:

Yields the largest value of *exponent* for the machine representation of the base type of P. The value of this attribute is of the type *universal_integer*. (See 13.7.3.)

P'MACHINE_EMIN   For a prefix P that denotes a floating-point type or subtype:

Yields the smallest (most negative) value of *exponent* for the machine representation of the base type of P. The value of this attribute is of the type *universal_integer*. (See 13.7.3.)

P'MACHINE_MANTISSA   For a prefix P that denotes a floating-point type or subtype:

Yields the number of digits in the *mantissa* for the machine representation of the base type of P (the digits are extended digits in the range 0 to P'MACHINE_RADIX -1). The value of this attribute is of the type *universal_integer*. (See 13.7.3.)

P'MACHINE_OVERFLOWS   For a prefix P that denotes a real type or subtype:

Yields the value TRUE if every predefined operation on values of the base type of P either provides a correct result or raises the exception NUMERIC_ERROR in overflow situations; yields the value FALSE otherwise. The value of this attribute is of the predefined type BOOLEAN. (See 13.7.3.)

P'MACHINE_RADIX   For a prefix P that denotes a floating-point type or subtype:

Yields the value of the *radix* used by the machine representation of the base type of P. The value of this attribute is of the type *universal_integer*. (See 13.7.3.)

P'MACHINE_ROUNDS   For a prefix P that denotes a real type or subtype:

Yields the value TRUE if every predefined arithmetic operation on values of the base type of P either returns an exact result or performs rounding; yields the value FALSE otherwise. The value of this attribute is of the predefined type BOOLEAN. (See 13.7.3.)

P'MANTISSA   For a prefix P that denotes a real subtype:

Yields the number of binary digits in the binary mantissa of model numbers of the subtype P. (This attribute yields the number B of section 3.5.7 for a floating-point type, or of section 3.5.9 for a fixed-point type.) The value of this attribute is of the type *universal_integer*. (See 3.5.8 and 3.5.10.)

P'POS   For a prefix P that denotes a discrete type or subtype:

This attribute is a function with a single parameter. The actual parameter X must be a value of the base type of P. The result type is the type *universal_inte-*

ger. The result is the position number of the value of the actual parameter. (See 3.5.5.)

P'POSITION   For a prefix P that denotes a component of a record object:

Yields the offset, from the start of the first storage unit occupied by the record, to the first of the storage units occupied by the component. This offset is measured in storage units. The value of this attribute is of the type *universal_integer*. (See 13.7.2.)

P'PRED   For a prefix P that denotes a discrete type or subtype:

This attribute is a function with a single parameter. The actual parameter X must be a value of the base type of P. The result type is the base type of P. The result is the value whose position number is one less than that of X. The exception CONSTRAINT_ERROR is raised if X equals P'BASE'FIRST. (See 3.5.5.)

P'RANGE   For a prefix P that is appropriate for an array type, or that denotes a constrained array subtype:

Yields the first index range of P, that is, the range P'FIRST .. P'LAST. (See 3.6.2.)

P'RANGE(N)   For a prefix P that is appropriate for an array type, or that denotes a constrained array subtype:

Yields the N-th index range of P, that is, the range P'FIRST(N) .. P'LAST(N). (See 3.6.2.)

P'SAFE_EMAX   For a prefix P that denotes a floating-point type or subtype:

Yields the largest exponent value in the binary canonical form of safe numbers of the base type of P. (This attribute yields the number E of section 3.5.7.) The value of this attribute is of the type *universal_integer*. (See 3.5.8.)

P'SAFE_LARGE   For a prefix P that denotes a real type or subtype:

Yields the largest positive safe number of the base type P. The value of this attribute is of the type *universal_real*. (See 3.5.8 and 3.5.10.)

P'SAFE_SMALL   For a prefix P that denotes a real type or subtype:

Yields the smallest positive (nonzero) safe number of the base type P. The value of this attribute is of the type *universal_real*. (See 3.5.8 and 3.5.10.)

P'SIZE   For a prefix P that denotes an object:

Yields the number of bits allocated to hold the object. The value of this attribute is of the type *universal_integer*. (See 13.7.2.)

P'SIZE   For a prefix P that denotes any type or subtype:

Yields the minimum number of bits that is needed by the implementation to hold any possible object of the type or subtype P. The value of this attribute is of the type *universal_integer*. (See 13.7.2.)

P'SMALL   For a prefix P that denotes a real subtype:

Yields the smallest positive nonzero) model number of the subtype P. The value of this attribute is of the type *universal_real*. (See 3.5.8 and 3.5.10.)

P'STORAGE_SIZE   For a prefix P that denotes an access type or
                 subtype:

Yields the total number of storage units reserved for the collection associated with the base type of P. The value of this attribute is of the type *universal_integer*. (See 13.7.2.)

P'STORAGE_SIZE   For a prefix P that denotes a task type or a task
                 object:

Yields the number of storage units reserved for each activation of a task of the type P or for the activation of the task object P. The value of this attribute is of the type *universal_integer*. (See 13.7.2.)

P'SUCC   For a prefix P that denotes a discrete type or subtype:

This attribute is a function with a single parameter. The actual parameter X must be a value of the base type of P. The result type is the base type of P. The result is the value whose position number is one greater than that of X. The exception CONSTRAINT_ERROR is raised if X equals P'BASE'LAST. (See 3.5.5.)

P'TERMINATED   For a prefix P that is appropriate for a task type:

Yields the value TRUE if the task P is terminated; yields the value FALSE otherwise. The value of this attribute is of the predefined type BOOLEAN. (See 9.9.)

P'VAL   For a prefix P that denotes a discrete type or subtype:

This attribute is a special function with a single parameter X which can be any integer type. The result type is the base type of P. The result is the value whose position number is the *universal_integer* value corresponding to X. The exception CONSTRAINT_ERROR is raised if the *universal_integer* value corresponding to X is not in the range P'POS(P'BASE'FIRST) .. P'POS(P'BASE' LAST). (See 3.5.5.)

P'VALUE   For a prefix P that denotes a discrete type or subtype:

This attribute is a function with a single parameter. The actual parameter X must be a value of the predefined type STRING. The result type is the base type of P. Any leading and any trailing spaces of the sequence of characters that corresponds to X are ignored.

For an enumeration type, if the sequence of characters has the syntax of an enumeration literal and if this literal exists for the base type of P, the result is the corresponding enumeration value. For an integer type, if the sequence of characters has the syntax of an integer literal, with an optional single leading character that is a plus or minus sign, and if there is a corresponding value in the base type of P, the result is this value. In any other case, the exception CONSTRAINT_ERROR is raised. (See 3.5.5.)

P'WIDTH   For a prefix that denotes a discrete subtype:

Yields the maximum image length over all values of the subtype P (the *image* is the sequence of characters returned by the attribute IMAGE). The value of this attribute is of the type *universal_integer*. (See 3.5.5.)

J

PREDEFINED
LANGUAGE PRAGMAS

This annex defines the pragmas LIST, PAGE, and OPTIMIZE, and summarizes the definitions given elsewhere of the remaining language-defined pragmas.

CONTROLLED

Takes the simple name of an access type as the single argument. This pragma is allowed only immediately within the declarative part or package specification that contains the declaration of the access type; the declaration must occur before the pragma. This pragma is not allowed for a derived type. This pragma specifies that automatic storage reclamation must not be performed for objects designated by values of the access type, except upon leaving the innermost block statement, subprogram body, or task body that encloses the access-type declaration, or after leaving the main program (see 4.8). [1]

ELABORATE

Takes one or more simple names denoting library units as arguments. This pragma is only allowed immediately after the context clause of a compilation unit (before the subsequent library unit or secondary unit). Each argument must be the simple name of a library unit mentioned by the context clause. This pragma specifies that the corresponding library unit body must be elaborated before the given compilation unit. If the given compilation unit is a subunit, the library unit body must be elaborated before the body of the ancestor library unit of the subunit (see 10.5).

INLINE

Takes one or more names as arguments; each name is either the name of a subprogram or the name of a generic subprogram. This pragma is allowed only

---

1 Cross references are for chapters and sections of the *Ada Language Reference Manual*. See note Appendix A.

at the place of a declarative item in a declarative part or package specification, or after a library unit in a compilation, but before any subsequent compilation unit. This pragma specifies that the subprogram bodies should be expanded inline at each call whenever possible; in the case of a generic subprogram, the pragma applies to calls of its instantiations (see 6.3.2).

INTERFACE

Takes a language name and a subprogram name as arguments. This pragma is allowed at the place of a declarative item, and must apply in this case to a subprogram declared by an earlier declarative item of the same declarative part or package specification. This pragma is also allowed for a library unit; in this case, the pragma must appear after the subprogram declaration, and before any subsequent compilation unit. This pragma specifies the other language (and thereby the calling conventions) and informs the compiler that an object module will be supplied for the corresponding subprogram (see 13.9).

LIST

Takes one of the identifiers ON or OFF as the single argument. This pragma is allowed anywhere a pragma is allowed. It specifies that listing of the compilation is to be continued or suspended until a LIST pragma with the opposite argument is given within the same compilation. The pragma itself is always listed if the compiler is producing a listing.

MEMORY_SIZE

Takes a numeric literal as the single argument. This pragma is allowed only at the start of a compilation, before the first compilation unit (if any) of the compilation. The effect of this pragma is to use the value of the specified numeric literal for the definition of the named number MEMORY_SIZE (see 13.9).

OPTIMIZE

Takes one of the identifiers, TIME or SPACE, as the single argument. This pragma is allowed only within a declarative part and it applies to the block or body enclosing the declarative part. It specifies whether time or space is the primary optimization criterion.

PACK

Takes the simple name of a record or array type as the single argument. The allowed positions for this pragma, and the restrictions on the named type, are governed by the same rules as for a representation clause. The pragma specifies that storage minimization should be the main criterion when selecting the representation of the given type (see 13.1).

PAGE

This pragma has no argument, and is allowed anywhere a pragma is allowed. It specifies that the program text that follows the pragma should start on a new page (if the compiler is currently producing a listing).

PRIORITY

Takes a static expression of the predefined integer subtype PRIORITY as the single argument. This pragma is allowed only within the specification of a task unit or immediately within the outermost declarative part of a main program. It specifies the priority of the task (or tasks of the task type) or the priority of the main program (see 9.8).

SHARED

Takes the simple name of a variable as the single argument. This pragma is allowed only for a variable declared by an object declaration, and whose type is a scalar or access type; the variable declaration and the pragma must both occur (in this order) immediately within the same declarative part or package specification. This pragma specifies that every read or update of the variable is a synchronization point for that variable. An implementation must restrict the objects for which this pragma is allowed to objects for which each of direct reading and direct updating is implemented as an indivisible operation (see 9.11).

STORAGE_UNIT

Takes a numeric literal as the single argument. This pragma is allowed only at the start of a compilation, before the first compilation unit (if any) of the compilation. The effect of this pragma is to use the value of the specified numeric literal for the definition of the named number STORAGE_UNIT (see 13.7).

SUPPRESS

Takes as arguments the identifier of a check and optionally also the name of either an object, a type or subtype, a subprogram, a task unit, or a generic unit. This pragma is allowed only either immediately within a declarative part or immediately within a package specification. In the latter case, the only allowed form is with a name that denotes an entity (or several overloaded subprograms) declared immediately within the package specification. The permission to omit the given check extends from the place of the pragma to the end of the declarative region associated with the innermost enclosing block statement or program unit. For a pragma given in a package specification, the permission extends to the end of the scope of the named entity.

If the pragma includes a name, the permission to omit the given check is further restricted: it is given only for operations on the named object or on all objects of the base type of a named type or subtype; for calls of a named subprogram; for activations of tasks of the named task type; or for instantiations of the given generic unit (see 11.7).

SYSTEM_NAME

Takes an enumeration literal as the single argument. This pragma is allowed only at the start of a compilation, before the first compilation unit (if any) of the compilation. The effect of this pragma is to use the enumeration literal with the specified identifier for the definition of the constant SYSTEM_NAME. This pragma is allowed only if the specified identifier corresponds to one of the literals of the type NAME declared in the package SYSTEM (see 13.7).

SYNTAX SUMMARY

```
abort_statement ::= abort task_name {, task_name};

accept_alternative ::=
    accept_statement [sequence_of_statements]

accept_statement ::=
    accept entry_simple_name [(entry_index)] [formal_part] [do
        sequence_of_statements
    end [entry_simple_name]];

access_type_definition ::= access subtype_indication

actual_parameter ::=
    expression | variable_name | type_mark(variable_name)

actual_parameter_part ::=
    (parameter_association {, parameter_association})

address_clause ::=
    for simple_name use at simple_expression;

alignment_clause ::= at mod static_simple_expression;

aggregate ::=
    (component_association {, component_association})

allocator ::=
    new subtype_indication | new qualified_expression

argument_association ::=
    [argument_identifier =>] name
  | [argument_identifier =>] expression

array_type_definition ::=
    unconstrained_array_definition | constrained_array_definition
```

```
assignment_statement ::=
    variable_name := expression;

attribute ::= prefix'attribute_designator

attribute_designator ::=
    simple_name [(universal_static_expression)]

base ::= integer

based_integer ::=
    extended_digit {[underline] extended_digit}

based_literal ::=
    base # based_integer [.based_integer] # [exponent]

basic_character ::=
    basic_graphic_character | format_effector

basic_declaration ::=
    object_declaration       | number_declaration
  | type_declaration         | subtype_declaration
  | subprogram_declaration   | package_declaration
  | task_declaration         | generic_declaration
  | exception_declaration    | generic_instantiation
  | renaming_declaration     | deferred_constant_declaration

basic_declarative_item ::= basic_declaration
  | representation_clause | use_clause

basic_graphic_character ::=
    upper_case_letter | digit
  | special_character | space_character

binary_adding_operator ::=  + | - | &

block_statement ::=
    [block_simple_name:]
       [declare
           declarative_part]
        begin
           sequence_of_statements
       [exception
           exception_handler
          {exception_handler}]
        end [block_simple_name];

body ::= proper_body | body_stub

body_stub ::=
    subprogram specification is separate;
  | package body package_simple_name is separate;
  | task body task_simple_name is separate;
```

```
case_statement ::=
    case expression is
        case_statement_alternative
        {case_statement_alternative}
    end case;

case_statement_alternative ::=
    when choice {| choice} =>
        sequence_of_statements

character_literal ::= 'graphic_character'

choice ::= simple_expression
  | discrete_range | others | component_simple_name

code_statement ::= type_mark'record_aggregate;

compilation ::= {compilation_unit}

compilation_unit ::=
    context_clause library_unit
  | context_clause secondary_unit

component_association ::=
    [choice {| choice} =>] expression

component_clause ::=
    component_name at static_simple_expression
                range static_range;

component_declaration ::=
    identifier_list : component_subtype_definition [:= expression]

component_list ::=
    component_declaration {component_declaration}
  | {component_declaration} variant_part
  | null;

component_subtype_definition ::= subtype_indication

compound_statement ::=
    if_statement      | case_statement
  | loop_statement    | block_statement
  | accept_statement  | select_statement

condition ::= boolean_expression

conditional_entry_call ::=
    select
        entry_call_statement
        [sequence_of_statements]
    else
        sequence_of_statements
    end select;

constrained_array_definition ::=
    array index_constraint of component_subtype_indication
```

```
constraint ::=
    range_constraint        | floating_point_constraint
  | fixed_point_constraint  | index_constraint
  | discriminant_constraint

context_clause ::= {with_clause {use_clause}}

decimal_literal ::= integer [.integer] [exponent]

declarative_part ::=
    {basic_declarative_item} {later_declarative_item}

deferred_constant_declaration ::=
    identifier_list : constant type_mark;

delay_alternative ::=
    delay_statement [sequence_of_statements]

delay_statement ::= delay simple_expression;

derived_type_definition ::= new subtype_indication

designator ::= identifier | operator_symbol

discrete_range ::= discrete_subtype_indication | range

discriminant_association ::=
    [discriminant_simple_name {| discriminant_simple_name} =>]
            expression

discriminant_constraint ::=
    (discriminant_association {, discriminant_association})

discriminant_part ::=
    (discriminant_specification {; discriminant_specification})

discriminant_specification ::=
    identifier_list : type_mark [:= expression]

entry_call_statement ::=
    entry_name [actual_parameter_part];

entry_declaration ::=
    entry identifier [(discrete_range)] [formal_part];

entry_index ::= expression

enumeration_literal ::= identifier | character_literal
enumeration_literal_specification ::= enumeration_literal

enumeration_representation_clause ::=
    for type_simple_name use aggregate;
```

```
enumeration_type_definition ::=
    (enumeration_literal_specification
      {, enumeration_literal_specification})

exception_choice ::= exception_name | others

exception_declaration ::= identifier_list : exception;

exception_handler ::=
    when exception_choice {| exception_choice} =>
        sequence_of_statements

exit_statement ::=
    exit [loop_name] [when condition];

exponent ::= E [+] integer | E - integer

expression ::=
    relation {and relation} | relation {and then relation}
  | relation {or relation}  | relation {or else relation}
  | relation {xor relation}

extended_digit ::= digit | letter

factor ::= primary [** primary] | abs primary | not primary

fixed_accuracy_definition ::=
    delta static_simple_expression

fixed_point_constraint ::=
    fixed_accuracy_definition [range_constraint]

floating_accuracy_definition ::=
    digits static_simple_expression

floating_point_constraint ::=
    floating_accuracy_definition [range_constraint]

formal_parameter := parameter_simple_name

formal_part ::=
    (parameter_specification {; parameter_specification})

full_type_declaration ::=
    type identifier [discriminant_part] is type_definition;

function_call ::=
    function_name [actual_parameter_part]
generic_actual_parameter ::= expression | variable_name
  | subprogram_name | entry_name | type_mark

generic_actual_part ::=
    (generic_association {, generic_association})
```

```
generic_association ::=
    [generic_formal_parameter =>] generic_actual_parameter

generic_declaration ::= generic_specification;

generic_formal_parameter ::=
    parameter_simple_name | operator_symbol

generic_formal_part ::= generic {generic_parameter_declaration}

generic_instantiation ::=
    package identifier is
        new generic_package_name [generic_actual_part];
  | procedure identifier is
        new generic_procedure_name [generic_actual_part];
  | function designator is
        new generic_function_name [generic_actual_part];

generic_parameter_declaration ::=
    identifier_list : [in [out]] type_mark [:= expression];
  | type identifier is generic_type_definition;
  | private_type_declaration
  | with subprogram_specification [is name];
  | with subprogram_specification [is <>];

generic_specification ::=
    generic_formal_part subprogram_specification
  | generic_formal_part package_specification

generic_type_definition ::=
    (<>) | range <> | digits <> | delta <>
  | array_type_definition | access_type_definition

goto_statement ::= goto label_name;

graphic_character ::= basis_graphic_character
  | lower_case_letter | other_special_character

highest_precedence_operator ::=  ** | abs | not

identifier :=
  letter {[underline] letter_or_digit}

identifier_list ::= identifier {, identifier}

if_statement ::=
      if condition then
          sequence_of_statements
    {elsif condition then
          sequence_of_statements}
    [else
          sequence_of_statements]
     end if;
```

```
incomplete_type_declaration ::=
    type identifier [discriminant_part];

index_constraint ::= (discrete_range {, discrete_range})

index_subtype_definition ::= type_mark range <>

indexed_component ::= prefix(expression {, expression})

integer ::= digit {[underline] digit}

integer_type_definition ::= range_constraint

iteration_scheme ::=  while condition
  | for loop_parameter_specification

label ::= <<label_simple_name>>

later_declarative_item ::= body
  | subprogram_declaration | package_declaration
  | task_declaration       | generic_declaration
  | use_clause             | generic_instantiation

length_clause ::= for attribute use simple_expression;

letter ::= upper_case_letter | lower_case_letter

letter_or_digit ::= letter | digit

library_unit ::=
    subprogram_declaration | package_declaration
  | generic_declaration    | generic_instantiation
  | subprogram_body

library_unit_body ::= subprogram_body | package_body

logical_operator ::= and | or | xor

loop_parameter_specification ::=
    identifier in [reverse] discrete_range

loop_statement ::=
    [loop_simple_name:]
      [iteration_scheme] loop
          sequence_of_statements
        end loop [loop_simple_name];
mode ::= [in] | in out | out

multiplying_operator ::=  * | / | mod | rem

name ::= simple_name
  | character_literal   | operator_symbol
  | indexed_component   | slice
  | selected_component  | attribute
```

```
null_statement ::= null;

number_declaration ::=
    identifier_list : constant := universal_static_expression;

numeric_literal ::= decimal_literal | based_literal

object_declaration ::=
    identifier_list : [constant] subtype_indication [:= expression];
  | identifier_list : [constant] constrained_array_definition
                                              [:= expression];

operator_symbol ::= string_literal

package_body ::=
    package body package_simple_name is
        [declarative_part]
    [begin
        sequence_of_statements
    [exception
        exception_handler
        {exception_handler}]]
    end [package_simple_name];

package_declaration ::= package_specification;

package_specification ::=
    package identifier is
        {basic_declarative_item}
    [private
        {basic_declarative_item}]
    end [package_simple_name]

parameter_association ::=
    [formal_parameter =>] actual_parameter

parameter_specification ::=
    identifier_list : mode type_mark [:= expression]

pragma ::=
    pragma identifier [(argument_association
                           {, argument_association})];

prefix ::= name | function_call

primary ::=
    numeric_literal | null | aggregate | string_literal
  | name | allocator | function_call | type_conversion
  | qualified_expression | (expression)

private_type_declaration ::=
    type identifier [discriminant_part] is [limited] private;
```

```
procedure_call_statement ::=
    procedure_name [actual_parameter_part];

proper_body ::=
    subprogram_body | package_body | task_body

qualified_expression ::=
    type_mark'(expression) | type_mark'aggregate

raise_statement ::= raise [exception_name];

range ::=  range_attribute
  | simple_expression .. simple_expression

range_constraint ::= range range

real_type_definition ::=
    floating_point_constraint | fixed_point_constraint

record_representation_clause ::=
    for type_simple_name use
        record [alignment_clause]
            {component_clause}
        end record;

record_type_definition ::=
    record
        component_list
    end record

relation ::=
    simple_expression [relational_operator simple_expression]
  | simple_expression [not] in range
  | simple_expression [not] in type_mark

relational_operator ::=  = | /= | < | <= | > | >=

renaming_declaration ::=
    identifier : type_mark       renames object_name;
  | identifier : exception       renames exception_name;
  | package identifier           renames package_name;
  | subprogram_specification     renames
                                 subprogram_or_entry_name;

representation_clause ::=
    type_representation_clause | address_clause

return_statement ::= return [expression];

secondary_unit ::= library_unit_body | subunit
```

```
select_alternative ::=
    [when condition =>]
        selective_wait_alternative

select_statement ::= selective_wait
  | conditional_entry_call | timed_entry_call

selected_component := prefix.selector

selective_wait ::=
      select
          select_alternative
    {or
          select_alternative}
    [else
          sequence_of_statements]
      end select;

selective_wait_alternative ::= accept_alternative
  | delay_alternative | terminate_alternative

selector ::= simple_name
    |  character_literal | operator_symbol | all

sequence_of_statements ::= statement { statement}

simple_expression ::=
      [unary_adding_operator] term {binary_adding_operator term}

simple_name ::= identifier

simple_statement ::= null_statement
  | assignment_statement | procedure_call_statement
  | exit_statement       | return statement
  | goto_statement       | entry_call_statement
  | delay_statement      | abort_statement
  | raise_statement      | code_statement

slice ::= prefix(discrete_range)

statement ::=
      {label} simple_statement | {label} compound_statement

string_literal ::= "{graphic_character}"

subprogram_body ::=
        subprogram_specification is
          [declarative_part]
        begin
           sequence_of_statements
      [exception
           exception_handler
           {exception_handler}]
        end [designator];
```

```
subprogram_declaration ::= subprogram_specification;

subprogram_specification ::=
    procedure identifier [formal_part]
  | function designator [formal_part] return type_mark

subtype_declaration ::=
    subtype identifier is subtype_indication;

subtype_indication ::= type_mark [constraint]

subunit ::= separate (parent_unit_name) proper_body

task_body ::=
    task body task_simple_name is
        [declarative_part]
    begin
        sequence_of_statements
    [exception
        exception_handler
        {exception_handler}
    end [task_simple_name];

task_declaration ::= task_specification;

task_specification ::=
    task [type] identifier [is
        {entry_declaration}
        {representation_clause}
    end [task_simple_name]]

term ::= factor {multiplying_operator factor}

terminate_alternative ::= terminate;

timed_entry_call ::=
    select
        entry_call_statement
        [sequence_of_statements]
    or
        delay_alternative
    end select;

type_conversion ::= type_mark(expression)

type_declaration ::= full_type_declaration
  | incomplete_type_declaration | private_type_declaration

type_definition ::=
    enumeration_type_definition | integer_type_definition
  | real_type_definition        | array_type_definition
  | record_type_definition      | access_type_definition
  | derived_type_definition
```

```
type_mark ::= type_name | subtype_name

type_representation_clause ::= length_clause
   | enumeration_representation_clause
   | record_representation_clause

unary_adding_operator ::=  + | -

unconstrained_array_definition ::=
     array (index_subtype_definition {, index_subtype_definition}) of
             component_subtype_indication

use_clause ::= use package_name {, package_name};

variant ::=
     when choice {| choice} =>
       component_list

variant_part ::=
     case discriminant_simple_name is
         variant
         {variant}
     end case;

with_clause ::=
     with unit_simple_name {, unit_simple_name};
```

BIBLIOGRAPHY

Gehani, 1987 Gehani, N. (1987) *UNIX Ada Programming*. Englewood Cliffs, NJ: Prentice-Hall.

Gonzalez, 1991 Gonzalez, D.W. (1991) *Ada Programmer's Handbook*. Reading, MA: Benjamin/Cummings.

LRM *Reference Manual for the Ada Programming Language* ANSI/MIL-STD-1815A. Washington, DC: American National Standards Institute, Inc.

Skansholm, 1988 Skansholm, J. (1988) *ADA FROM THE BEGINNING*. Reading, MA: Addison-Wesley.

Watt, 1987 Watt, D.A., Wichmann, B.A., and Findlay, W.F. (1987) *ADA Language and Methodology*. Englewood Cliffs, NJ: Prentice Hall International.

INDEX

" (quotation marks), string literal enclosing symbol, 14–15
& (ampersand), concatenation operator, 22, 43
' (apostrophe)
   attribute delimiter, 23, 24, 27, 41–42, 107
   character literal enclosing symbol, 14
* (asterisk), multiplication operator, 19–20
** (double asterisk), exponentiation operator, 19–20
\+ (plus sign)
   addition operator, 19
   plus operator, 19
\- (minus sign)
   minus operator, 19
   subtraction operator, 19–20
. (period), name delimiter, 45, 74, 90, 100
-- (double hyphen), comment symbol, 3, 15
/ (slash)
   division operator, 19–20
   null indicator, 64
/= (not equal sign), inequality operator, 21
:= (colon/equal sign), assignment operator, 29
; (semicolon), statement terminator, 4, 29
< (less than sign), less operator, 21
<= (less than or equal sign), less/equal operator, 21
<> (box), default designator, 83
(<>) ((box)), parameter-type designator, 82
= (equal sign), equality operator, 21

> (greater than sign), greater operator, 22
>= (greater than or equal sign), greater/equal operator, 22
[] (square brackets), optional item symbols, 12
{} (braces), zero or more repetitions symbols, 12
| (vertical bar), alternative choices symbol, 12

abnormal tasks, 107
abort statements, 37, 107
absolute value (operation), 19
abs operator, 19
abstract data types (ADTs), 78
accept alternatives. *See* **accept** statements
accept statements, 100–101, 102–4
`Access_Check` run-time check, 116
access errors, 111
access-type literals, 64
access types, 18, 54, 63–72, 82, 98
access variables, 63, 65–66
   assignments to, 66–67
   comparing, 65
   deallocation of, 72
   declaring, 66–67
   initialization of, 64
   See also allocation of dynamic variables; dynamic variables
actual parameters, 53–54, 56, 79, 84
Ada
   basic structure, 1–4
   process communication in, 97
   program-listing conventions, 2
Ada data types. *See* data types
Ada Language Reference Manual. *See Language Reference Manual (LRM)*

Ada reserved words, listed, 119
addition, 19–20
addition operator (+), 19–20
`'Address` attribute, 143
ADTs. *See* abstract data types (ADTs)
`'Aft` attribute, 143
aggregates. *See* array aggregates; record aggregates
algorithms, for generic units, 79
allocation of dynamic variables, 64–66
   with qualified_expressions, 65–66
   with subtype_indications, 64–65
   See also access variables; dynamic variables; **new** allocator
.all references, 64
alternative choices symbol (|), 12
ampersand (&), concatenation operator, 22, 43
and operator, 22, 24–25
and then operator, 22, 25–26
ANSI/MIL-STD-1815A, Reference Manual for the Ada Programming Language. See Language Reference Manual (LRM)
apostrophe (')
   attribute delimiter, 23, 24, 27, 41–42, 107
   character literal enclosing symbol, 14
arithmetic operations, 19–20
arithmetic operators, 19–20
array aggregates, 41
array assignments, 40–41
array attributes, 41–43
array components, 39–43
array indexes, 39–42
array objects, 40